The Angel's Earring

Healing through Dreams and Creativity

Vicki Lynn Milnark

THE ANGEL'S EARRING
Healing through Dreams and Creativity

ISBN 978-0-578-68809-1

Cover art: Copy of Abbott Handerson Thayer's "Angel, 1887," oil on canvas held by the Smithsonian American Art Museum

Manufactured in the United States of America
First printing June 2020

DEDICATION

This book is dedicated to my partner, Gene, who valued and supported my many hours at the computer; my sons, Jason and Nate; my grandchildren, Martin, Emily, Riley, Brianna, Myla, and Mason; and my brother, Matt, whose love inspired me to continue until publication.

ACKNOWLEDGEMENTS

Remembering and recording dreams is a solitary ritual. Painting, drawing, and writing similarly are accomplished alone. Yet, there are many teachers and mentors who assisted me along the way. Some instructors stand out in creative writing, drawing, and ceramics whose names I unfortunately do not recall. They nonetheless remain in my psyche. In a human development class a professor by the name of Dr. Patricia McCullough called me to say I had written the best paper in the class. She supported my continued efforts. I thank her. She, too, is still with me.

In my art therapy training, the professors at Ursuline College were my people. I loved and learned greatly from the late Sr. Kathleen Burke, OSU, PhD, ATR-BC; Amy Jacobs, ATR-BC, PhD; Gail Rule-Hoffman, M.Ed., LPC-S, ATR-BC, LICDC-S; and Diane Meros, ATR-BC. Similarly, I want to recognize Mickie McGraw, ATR-BC. She founded the oldest medical art therapy studio in the country at Metro Hospital in Cleveland, OH. She supervised me and did the initial read of my book. Because of her, I pared it down from two books to one. Similarly, I wish to thank Martha Stitt, ATR-BC, LPC-S, for her role in supervision.

Although I do not know the two following people personally, I want to thank Shaun McNiff, PhD, ATR-BC, for his role as an educator and for his kind assistance in answering publishing questions, and Pat B. Allen, PhD, ATR, for her role as an author. She inspired my writing in *Art is a Way of Knowing:*

A Guide to Self-Knowledge and Spiritual Fulfillment through Creativity. Thanks also for her help in answering publishing questions.

Furthermore, I wish to acknowledge my friend, Jennifer Zgonc, LPC-S, who edited the first draft of my book. She has supported and encouraged me greatly. Similarly, I honor John Troyer, LPC, whom I met through his Jungian book discussion group. He gave me feedback on some chapters, encouraged me to continue when I felt downhearted, and assisted me by asking two of his friends for comments of the same material. Most importantly, I have the greatest appreciation for art therapist and author Lucia Capacchione. She not only read my book, but she also endorsed it, and offered support beyond measure in the publishing and marketing process. I am forever in her debt.

CONTENTS

LIST OF FIGURES

25. "Selves over Time"
26. "Eve"
27. "Little People"
28. "Soma"
29. "Floating"
30. "Wasteland"
31. "Saturn"
32. "The Bull"
33. "Kabbalah Mandala"
34. "The Magician" (Waite-Rider deck)
35. "Whirlwind"
36. "Child"
37. "Pisces Rotated"
38. "Future Goldfish"
39. "Round Fish"
40. "The Three Graces"
41. "Artist Trading Card" (2007), after the Goddess of Laussel; 22,000–18,000 BC
42. "Mary of the Watery Moon Float"
43. "Mary of Lourdes Float"
44. "Indigenous Dancers," Ajijic, Mexico
45. "Rosemary"
46. "Vajrayogini"
47. "Giraffe Totem: Stand tall in your inquisitive instinct."
48. "Creative Heart"
49. "Wheel Flower"

PREFACE

As a single, young mother, I turned to dreams, art, poetry, and the writings of Carl Jung for solace. He believed we have a "Great Man" within, a Self. In my case, she is a "Great Woman." A voice spoke in meditation and sometimes dreams and art. For many years she attempted to warn me, but I was rebellious or did not believe I had intuition. Therefore, I ignored the inner promptings, especially with the men I dated who confirmed my unworthiness. On the other hand, when I returned to art again, she spoke with an intensity I could no longer ignore. I was not making it up and knew I must make changes.

Those around me say my thoughts are deep and difficult to understand. Not until recently did I find I was an intuitive type from my analyst. At first, I contemplated this book to be an art therapy guide for the general readership. The book furthermore is intended as a path toward spiritual healing. However, *The Angel's Earring* is probably better suited for those who have a background in Jung, psychology, mythology, or mysticism. Jung, too, was cryptic, and his trained analysts still argue about his terms and concepts. Therefore, please bear with me. I tried to define his concepts as best I could.

Jung wrote in a circular style, like my own. I cannot work from an outline or plan a work of art. My creativity is intuitive and feeling first, then I organize the chaos. I have attempted in this organization to arrange poetry, dreams, and images according to themes or states of mind present in my direct experience. This included many, many revisions. I repeatedly wanted to give up, feeling depressed and overwhelmed with the details. All the while, however, synchronicities and dreams validated my work even if others did not, because of my style.

In my work as an art therapist, I similarly asked the client questions based on my intuition. However, I did not interpret. Yet I could see how art revealed and healed sexual trauma, for example. Clients do not want to remember, and have often been threatened that, if they told, they would be killed. They are also deeply ashamed as if they "asked for it." But the images cannot lie. They call out for emotions to be expressed. *Something* within wants the artist to be healed.

I observed emotional expression, for example, when working at an eating disorders intensive outpatient program. Clients with anorexia, for example, restrict food and emotions to not gain weight. The behavior of restriction is an internal repression of feelings. Art will not allow this. Colors and lines spray on the surface of paper. Moreover, the art connected clients in my groups and helped them overcome fears and to grow. Similar symbols emerged, displaying the connection perhaps from the collective unconscious. The experience felt like oneness. But here again, the image holds so many meanings; the interpretation cannot be limited to words. Furthermore, this extends to images in dreams. We can only guess and make associations that are particular to the individual.

Jung was asked on television if he believed in God. He answered, "I don't believe, I know." Yet the image of God is not like the one on the Sistine Chapel. Jung had his own vision of God. He experienced it. I also am convinced there is something. Whatever the mystery is, I cannot know. But my work with dreams and art has brought me joy, peace, and confidence. My hope is that it can also deepen the reader's connection with Self.

I anticipate that readers of this book might wish to employ art and dreams in personal and professional contexts. For example, art and dreams can be included by using journals outside of session to be explored during it. In my experience, this work cuts through denial because words often get in the way. Furthermore, I encourage readers to experiment with the methods shown here and to obtain further training in art therapy or at a Jungian center. In these ways, your own spiritual development will likewise progress.

Lastly, but as importantly, the weight and responsibility of these explorations may belong to those of us with privilege. One must first survive and be in a space of safety before there is time and even the means for deep reflection and personal growth. Yet, on the other hand, everyone dreams, and anyone can make art. As I have seen in my art therapy groups, no higher education is needed, nor do people need to read the Collective Works to find meaning from the images. We all can become the artists of our own lives.

INTRODUCTION

Shame and introversion kept me silent most of my life, without stories. Yet off in a dark, lonely place at the top of the world, she saved me. Like the north star, she guided me through wounds, into a liminal universe. I could hear her in the rhythms of the moon, the rain, and the whispering leaves. She opened my eyes by glinting off water. In nature's stillness, I was with her. Yet when my feet sunk deep in mud or my legs, twisted and leaden refusing movement, she transformed me. I could hear her growl through my ancestors. In an attic trunk, she hid animal masks. Inside and out she broadened me, but only after fifteen years of creativity and another fifteen years to contemplate. Not only did she never judge or leave me, but she also gave me an inner family and knowing. Because of her, I will never be alone again.

In northern Finland, Norway, Sweden, and parts of Russia, the Sámi people reside in a vast landscape, called Sampi, near and above the Arctic Circle. According to archeologists, this culture originally lived near the Ural Mountains in Russia and were driven there by other, more aggressive tribes. Artifacts indicate they arrived in Norway about 9000 BC.[1] However, the Sámi were displaced due to war and intruded upon by farmers many times. Some Sámi people still practice healing or shamanism, although original forms were subverted due to Christianity. Sometimes they become ecstatic and journey to spirit worlds or contact the ancestors to heal and restore balance. They use ritual implements like the drum and hammer. Some dress in costume and wear star-shaped, pointed hats. Furthermore, the Sámi worship a pantheon of gods, like Beaivi, goddess of the sun, gods for days of the week, and gods who watched over families. Gods of disease and of the underworld, however, were also part of the pantheon. The Sámi worship bears. They exalt ancestors. Although they fish, trap and farm, most Sámi are semi-nomadic herders, especially of reindeer.[2] They have gifts.

These gifts arrive when scholars trace words backward to those times writing emerged. The study is called etymology. Therefore, the origin of the word *Sámi* likely was borrowed from the Proto-Finnic word *Hame* or *Sama*, also *Suomi*, which means "Finland." In turn, a Proto-Germanic word, *soma,* is related to the Baltic word *zeme,* meaning "land." The Sámi are mentioned in Norse sagas and the Icelandic Eddas. Sámi, as a word, is also derived from Old Norse, *finna*, from proto-Germanic, *finthian* ("to find"). The Sámi and shamankas are hunters.[3] So are dreamers, poets, and artists. In any case, in my dreams and art, I followed a bear, as well as other animals. We ate honey. First hear the images; then look to words.

I owe this heritage to my Finnish grandmother, Sarah. Her father, Sanfried Jacobsen, was from Alavieska, Finland. He married Annie Maki about 1904 after emigrating to Canada in 1896. His parents were the Wuotilas. While I am unsure if any of my Finnish ancestors were Sámi, Alavieska is not far from Lapland. I mention all this because I, too, venerate my ancestors and visited Oulu, Finland in 2019. Oulu is about an hour from Alavieska.

Inhabitants of Finland tend to be stoic, addicted, and depressed. When you pass them on the street and smile, you get no response. They drink beer or gin and grapefruit at breakfast in airports. But if they see you with a map, they will help with directions. Apart from these curiosities, the land felt sacred. Maybe it was the pure air, the white birch groves, the art, or design that captured me. The area was not overcrowded; nor did people seem rushed. Bicycle paths webbed one area to the next. An elementary school was situated next to a forest. One path led my partner and I from Oulu across islands to Nallikari Beach on the Baltic Sea. Moreover, Hupisaaret Island Park combined a botanical garden, a lake with fountains, and a local history museum. In it, I learned how the men made tar for a living. Maybe this is how my great-grandfather survived prior to emigration. In my bones, I felt I belonged there. Although my mother said I was 25 percent Finnish, the genes of my grandmother are strong in our family. For example, my mom and uncle, my two brothers, my son, and myself are all introverts. And many of us are blonde and resemble Finns.

Anyway, I kept the stories quiet. We do not speak openly about the mysteries because we are intended to be hunters. Therefore, we are meant to sniff the scent, to reflect, find meaning, to dream. In the upper world, I was mostly a divorced mother, anxious and depressed. Although I worked a responsible job to support my children, I was strangely attracted to abusive men. Repeatedly. My picker was broken, my minister told me. Was she saying I was a failure as a wife? My mind also said my parenting was deficient. No one wants to utter these sagas.

When my youngest went off to college, I landed in a cavern, with a thud, sobbing. No longer a mother and not engaged in a meaningful career, I was without identity. My soul knew my career as a nuclear medicine technologist was not my calling. Although I did look inside at how my patients' bodies were functioning and continued to explore my inner self, I did not want to know I was depressed or to hear the instructions of this state of soul.

Nonetheless the images, my angels (were they also radiologists?), showed me so I could not deny it any longer.

They knitted together my fragments into a stronger sense of self, mirroring my emotions so I could give them names. Oddly, by sleeping and paying attention to dreams, the dreams woke me up. My creative forms, poetry, drawings, paintings, and ceramics, too, guided me so I could hear her call and let go of the security my employment afforded me.

She told me to paint as just a voice in a dream. This was the first flicker of movement. When I dove seriously into the depths by painting dreams, the images tried to drown me. For example, I painted a fearsome character. He abducted and ripped me apart in the underworld for years, but I didn't give up. He stalked me in garages and parking lots. But as a helper, this dream character revealed my self-hatred. Consequently, I knocked him down, shedding the role of victim.

As if these experiences weren't enough, a dark, feminine presence arrived. Maybe she was Persephone, abducted by Hades, lord of the dead, when she was raped. Or was the figure Eve, Sophia, goddess of wisdom? Moreover, the black goddess arises in Song of Songs in the Old Testament. She is the Shulamite, who similarly is black and beautiful. On the other hand, Kali, a Hindu goddess, is also black with a necklace of skulls. Nude, she dances on her spouse, Shiva. Although Kali shocks and destroys, her brown underworld also contains dwarfs. They are miners. The angel of painting led me to their treasures.

Dying numerous times so I could see, so I could hear differently, I shot up from captivity as a headless mother holding a baby cactus. Furthermore, I did the unimaginable to give my soul a drink. From a straw, I sipped a baby's brains. Perhaps headhunters of the past, who also lapped the brains of their victims, were active inside. Carl Jung said we all have a three-million-year-old human inside. Therefore, images link us to prehistoric times as well as the symbolism of what is happening now. Such is the feminine wisdom of soma, a hallucinogen imbibed in mystery cults. Along with Kali, Soma is a Hindu, feminine goddess. Where would Soma have me land or hunt next, I wondered. Maybe in Finland, according to the root meanings of Sami I mentioned earlier. Yet I knew I needed to accept sacrifice voluntarily so I could serve the Self.

This was a dusky, moist time of tears. Maybe the Greek myth of Kronos, who ate his own children, lived in me. Kronos was an early Greek god, a jealous Titan, who envied his own father's power. He was a watcher who was overthrown by his son, Zeus. Rhea saved Zeus at birth by offering Kronos, her mate, a stone. We think of Kronos as Father Time. In Roman mythology, Kronos was called Saturn and was related to the planet. Moreover, Saturn's influence included limits and depression, although he is also god of agriculture and conformity. He is sometimes pictured with a scythe and turns fields to stubble. I didn't want to meet him.

Nonetheless, I was laid out to dry in the desert where I wrestled with her. She broke my hip. I don't recall, but I must have asked for a blessing before I made my travail. She tricked me many times and disappeared. Yet here, I had a glimpse of her as the Shekinah, the feminine dwelling place of God. She supplied a tent. It was magical. Or was it just an apparition? Nonetheless, she left me alone in that dry, dusty climate, where the Great Father judged and burned me for what felt like an eon. Incubation and purification, on and on, I waited. Perhaps I was hunting the dragon to kill it. Was I stalking the parental complexes to gain the assistance of the Great Mother and Father? A shamanka, a seeker, asks too many questions. Yet even here, sometimes rain produces flowers.

The hunt, however, still wasn't over. I needed to die again to be resurrected. Near Jerusalem in the dark, where a cookfire burned, I was with other wanderers. Here they also witnessed the pulsating heart thumping in a living skeleton cow. So did others. I sold the painting. La Loba, the Bone Woman, must be at hand. According to stories from Northern Mexico, she fleshes out bones, Clarissa Estés points out. La Loba, therefore, resurrects the dead, especially the wolf. Maybe the wolf, the Bone Woman, and bull run free outside Jerusalem, reminding women of her connection to the Great Goddess. Some 20,000 years ago, statues and other figures show her riding on the back of a bull who later became her son-lover. Sometimes when we look to the past, we can be reborn.

The material in this book was a long gestational period. It was a metamorphosis through Christianity, Gnosticism, Judaism, Neopaganism, Alchemy, Buddhism, shamanism, mask, and myth. The angel opened a divine portal of energy through religious images. From the collective unconscious archetypes made visitations, seizing me and whipping up whirlwinds. From the vortex she coughed up a grandmother, child, fish, daughter, and inner minister. I squeezed her from hidden places onto the paper or canvas or clay shape. She installed grace. She led me to the rose garden so I could bloom a vocation. At the age of fifty, I came into my own.

To gain some understanding of unconscious material, I grouped dreams by recurring themes and images chronologically as best I could. More importantly, the arrangement is under headings of spiritual experiences I traversed stamped by images and poems I created along the way. My intention was to amplify messages from dreams so I could better hear them. My wish is to offer you a pilgrimage from pain to peace. Eight chapters investigate how I circled my inner mountain. The ninth chapter is about methods of healing I used and continue to use because I know our development continues evermore. Entertain periods of silence. Create. Listen. Track her. You can be a seeker too.

CHAPTER 1: AWAKENING THE SLEEPING BEAUTY

"The world – so far as it has not completely turned its back on tradition – has long ago stopped wanting to hear a 'message'; it would rather be told what the message means."[4]

My story begins with Swiss psychiatrist Carl Jung. He originally was trained by Freud but formed his own psychology of the unconscious. Because he was married to a wealthy woman, he didn't financially need to see many patients. Therefore, he had plenty of time to think, study the ancients, write, paint, and use his imagination. I'd describe Jung as a contemporary mystic, genius, and prophet. In *Memories, Dreams, Reflections*, for example, he writes about his visions prior to World War I, of blood covering the European continent. Connected to a dimension most people are unaware, called the collective unconscious, he gathered facts to confirm his experiences and those of his patients. More significantly, he reinterpreted what being Christian meant. He knew Christ exists within and that the Holy Ghost in our age incarnates, perhaps as feminine. Jung additionally taught we don't have to be a saint to enter a relationship with the Self; we need wholeness. What follows is the story of how I became aware of the unconscious by investigating dreams, the Grail symbol as crater, creating self-expressive images, hearing the call to vocation, and client art therapy images.

Come with me on this mystery tour. Instead of just believing what you were taught, have faith you can *know*. We hold fast to our beliefs, fearing lightning will strike us dead if we let go. If I don't stay with the faith that I was born into from a divine figure long ago, passed down generation by generation, I may become the victim of the devil or a false teacher, I was told. The divine only speaks to the chosen ones, like Jesus, Buddha, Mohammed. I'm too sinful, so I should just pray, attend the church, synagogue, mosque, or temple and listen to the priest, rabbi, or imam. All is written in the sacred word. But what if your very own dreams are a call to participate in the eternal? What if the divine wants you just as much as you long for him or her?

In the Gospel of Miryam, or Mary, considered a fifth-century Gnostic text disallowed in the Christian canon, the Messiah implores us to likewise search. Below the term "human child" refers to the Son of Man:

> Peace be with you, receive my peace. Take care
> That no one send you lost into the wrong,
> Saying, "Look over here," or "Look over there."
> The human child exists in you. Follow
> The Child. And if you look you'll find the child.
> Go out and preach the message of good news
> About the kingdom. Don't seek any rules
> Other than what I give you. Establish
> No law as lawgivers have done, or by
> Those laws each one of you will end up bound.[5]

When I began, I was tied up in knots, not knowing what I was tracking or how long it would take to have some glimmer of freedom. Although I appeared fully functional, with a job, home, and family, a friend of mine was on to me. After I saw her in tears graduating from nursing school, she asked, "Don't you ever feel anything?" My blank face only scoured the floor. Another person, a stranger, echoed this idea. He stopped me in a crowded mall and asked if I was okay. Although I answered, "Oh, I'm fine," as I looked up, I wasn't at all. Holding on to terrible beliefs about myself left me incredibly shaky.

Prior to hearing the call, many of us start off ruminating, planning, buying, working, eating, to stop the panic. We think all the things we don't have will save us. We look for happiness in relationships. Our heads are filled with all these notions of who we think we need to be and where we need to go to find satisfaction. Perfectionism wields its ugly head, but we don't hear the inner chatter and don't feel the feelings. I had no idea I was controlled by the characters and stories just below the surface. Frantic activity didn't still the cacophony; didn't create a life worth living. Instead, I threw pieces of myself to the winds.

I gave away my power by believing I was unlovable. When young, I, like an antenna, attracted partners who were abusive, had mental difficulties, or addictions. After two divorces and a third romantic partner, I still didn't learn from my mistakes. How was I to know? Something felt familiar. A part of me blocked signs others could see. My eyes only saw what my story or karma created because I was sleeping under a spell, a repetition compulsion. But there was a payoff. I became the long-suffering martyr. This identity gave me stories to tell my women friends, mostly about how I had been wronged, how cruel my spouse or boyfriend had been. As the martyr, I rose up as if on a cross and got to look down on these culprits. I didn't do anything to change myself, but I did get to gossip a lot. This identity didn't serve me. Before this decision, I imitated my mother and agreed to the recipes of life given by biology. As women, we are in accord with images of self-sacrifice, to live for others as unaware women often do. This is not what the angel wants even if it is our genetic and cultural role to nurture others. A war between passivity and action raged within. I waited for a prince and dreamt of becoming a scientist or an artist. The opposition of my aim and the feminine need to be in relationship clashed.

Like the depressed person I'd become, other artists and writers, I found, entered the cave, the dark wood, or underworld, too. For example, artist Pablo Picasso had a blue period reflected in his paintings after a friend died. Artist Paul Cézanne's portfolio included dark works before feelings of liberation lighted up his authentic style. The poet, Dante, additionally encountered levels of hell before finding his Divine Rose. Images of darkness and death pervade Jungian psychologist Clarissa Pinkola Estés' accounts of women's early dreams. Even in meditation, psychologist Lawrence LeShan in *How to Meditate* warns that the first images might include bones, death, and dismemberment at first. When we dream, paint, or meditate, we encounter soul's darkness. As an initiation, it must be endured to develop hearing.

Memory is so very odd. The older I become, the more elusive. We know certain tricks that aid recall; for me it was painting or drawing an experience. One dream, prior to the cave I entered, was about a colorful comforter wafting down into a crater. Of course, I had no idea what the image meant and the only reason I recall it is that I painted it. Decades later, however, I put on my Sherlock hat and began to investigate the meaning of the word *crater.* Its etymology traced back to when words were first written. For example, *crater* in Latin meant "mixing bowl"; from Greek *kratEr;* from *kerannynai* "to mix"; akin to Sanskrit *srlnAti,* "he mixes," the bowl-shaped depression around the orifice of a volcano; a depression formed by an impact of a meteorite; a hole in the ground made by the explosion of a bomb or shell; an eroded lesion; a dimple in a painted surface.[6]

Often the first phase of individuation occurs with suffering and the wounding of the person. Both a shock and a call to find our center, it usually is not acknowledged.[7] Was this dream a wounding, or was my chaotic outer life a series of them? It was like I was a fool, a person without wisdom yet searching for it internally. According to Katherine Tingley, "The word theosophy is derived from the Greek theo-sophia, which means 'divine wisdom.'"[8] I. M. Oderberg, a theosophical writer, further states *crater* was the Greco-Italian word for "vessel" that later evolved to the word "grail" in English. The author adds the "vessel being the means of the attainment of 'atonement' of the 'child' or human being with its 'Father' or source of existence." In the remainder of the article, Oderberg writes about the quest for the Grail in the legend of Parzifal.[9] Perhaps therefore, this dream was an initiation marking the quest for my own center.

Similarly, Jung says the crater is part of alchemy and Gnosticism. As you may know, the alchemists on the surface were trying to turn lead into gold by various chemical processes. The lead is sometimes referred to as the beginning state, or chaos in wait of transformation. Jung cites Zosimos, a hermetic gnostic, who wrote about the "crater" as a transformative vessel hastening the process of alchemy. It was like a baptismal font filled with a sort of dignifying dye, sent by God to man, "who wished to free himself from his natural, imperfect, sleeping state" (perhaps represented by lead) of unawareness with "an opportunity to dip himself in the *nous* and thus partake of the higher state" of consciousness.[10] Gnosticism was an early Jewish-Christian set of ideas. Gnostics believed humans have a divine spark trapped in their bodies that could be liberated by *gnosis*, a knowing from direct experience. In Gnosticism, *nous* means "mind." Therefore, the crater served as a "place" mind might rest, a container for it.

My dream, however, also had a "comforter" reclining in the crater. When I think of comfort, a quilt, or making comfortable, the feminine is implied. But there is more. If we study the meanings of the word *comforter* in a spiritual way, we can look to John 14:26 (KJV) for a reference. "But the Comforter, which is the Holy Ghost, whom the Father will send in my name, he shall teach you all things, and bring all things to your remembrance, whatsoever I have said unto you." Also, John 14:16; 15:26; and 16:7 say the Comforter was a designation for the Holy Ghost. Yet more importantly, John 16:7 says, " Nevertheless I tell you the truth. It is expedient for you that I go away: for if I go not away, the Comforter will not come unto you; but if I depart, I will send him unto you."

Although there is debate about the gender of the Holy Spirit, Dutch academic Johannes van Oort writes the first to worship Jesus were Jewish Christians. They referred to the Holy Spirit as Mother. "An essential background to the occurrence of the Holy Spirit as Mother is, of course, the fact that the Hebrew word for Spirit, *ruach*, is in nearly all cases feminine. The first Christians, all of whom were Jews, took this over. Also, in Aramaic the word for Spirit, *rucha*, is feminine." Other early texts refer to the Holy Spirit as the mother of Christ, an angel, as Wisdom, and as the "old woman."[11]

The crater and comforter are symbols but may represent archetypes. I believe archetypes show up in dreams as landscapes, objects, animals, or yet are personified in people we know or don't specifically know. Author M. Esther Harding writes that in Jungian psychology they are primordial, universal images that create an imprint on the psyche.[12] Jung, for example, initially found archetypal images in patients with schizophrenia. I remember him writing about one such person who thought he was seeing the sun with a tube extending from it. Jung found the image from a book of some myth or Egyptian god, I think. The patient had no previous knowledge of the image, yet Egyptians certainly had. Archetypes are not concrete, black-and-white, fully explainable things, but are unseen energies operating inside the individual sometimes from the unpleasant pole, sometimes from the pleasant. They assist in restoring balance and encourage enlargement of the personality, called individuation. They speak through images. In my case, a crater and a comforter. They strive to be known.

Contents of the unconscious arise in ways other than dreams to awaken us. Associations often lead to unconscious elements that have been repressed or assimilated without choice. Whereas Freud used a chain of associations, Jung would stick to the image; that is, never going more than a word or phrase away. He also viewed each element in the dream as a part of the self, arising from the personal unconscious and what he called the collective unconscious. The personal unconscious might be thought as being like the right brain. It is wordless but contains a multitude of images and emotions from our personal past, whereas the left brain is verbal and logical. The collective unconscious, however, Jung instructs, is a receptacle of myths, rituals, and images of all beings going back to more than a million years ago. Although most dreams are simply contents of the personal unconscious, related to mother, father, and other complexes, even these are lower manifestations of archetypes. American psychologist James Hillman influenced me by the word *personification,* how divinities inhabit the costumes of ordinary people in dreams. Therefore, I looked at the characteristics of people for their mythic roles, although this may not be the way a Jungian analyst would work with a dream in a session.

Other than dreams, art had given me solace in high school, so I made my return to it looking for purpose, a way out of my misery. I enrolled in art classes and drew still life, then life drawing, then painting. Drawing jump-started the new vision I began to have of me, breaking up the bleakness. Out of that gray flat humdrum, artistic pursuit opened my eyes to a new world alive with emerging textures, shadows, and variations of color I never realized. Apparently, depression collapsed me and my surroundings into nothing but a gray, flat blur. The beauty, complexity, and variety of the newly seen landscape swept into my inner world by way of the senses. The expressiveness of the human body as a conversion of an alive three-dimensional being into a two-dimensional format gives presence to something beyond what you know or intend.

Part of my depression stemmed from my job at the time. I was a nuclear medicine technician. While it allowed me to raise my children, it wasn't my passion. My career identity – an artist or an art therapist – formed over something like ten years. I contacted an art therapy program for requirements and enrolled in art classes but was scared to commit. I recall one radiologist telling me I was crazy to give up a twenty-five-dollar-an-hour job at my age for a ten-dollar-an-hour one. Because of a protracted refusal to listen to the call, my drawings, paintings, and ceramics span a time, from about 1991 to 2001, the height occurring from 1993 to 1995. Ceramics was the last requirement needed for the art therapy program, and I stalled again, taking more classes than I needed. After all, my professor was so inspiring, I told myself. He, for example, said that a piece contained three parts – the artist, the object chosen to sculpt, and a third, something that would tell the artist what the piece needed. As I look back, perhaps I was dallying with the Lover archetype rather than moving forward to a new career. Why not? Maybe this is what I needed to do.

The Lover archetype, authors Thomas L. Moore and Douglas Gillette say, represents the divine life force itself.

The Lover's energy is about passion, spiritual hunger, and sensuality. Or we can think of this archetype as a princess to include the feminine. Play, exhibition, aesthetics, relatedness to nature, celebrating the body without shame, and compassion for others are qualities of the Greek god Eros and of the Lover. The authors also say the Lover resides in the collective unconscious and may be the signal to mysticism. On the other hand, this archetype installs not only exuberance and joy but profound grief. All the arts, as in painting, poetry, music, dance, and drama, are inspired from this archetype. He opposes the norm and the law.[13] I will talk about this in a dream later.

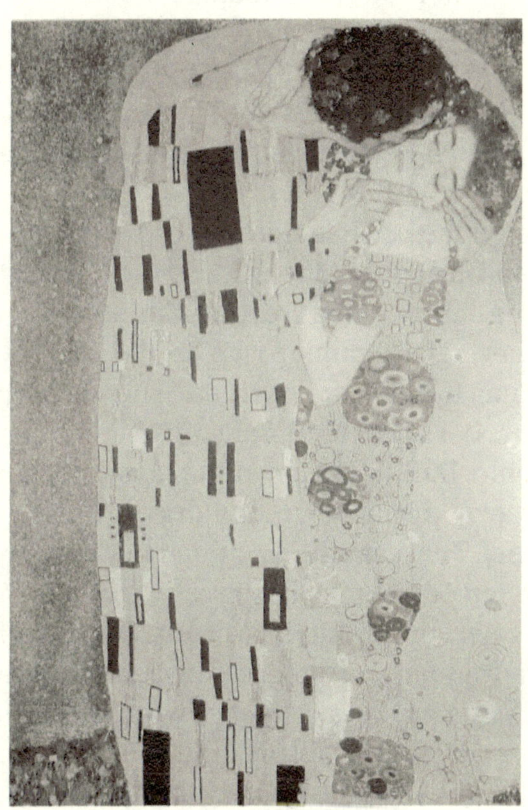

Figure 1. "The Kiss"

My favorite painting, "The Kiss" by Gustav Klimt, located in the Austrian Gallery Belvedere, displays the shimmering golden pattern of the Lover. At the time I viewed it, I hadn't digested the extended energies of Eros. I simply loved the painting and all of Klimt's figures, by the way. He paints awe-inspiring women and has a striking style. I saw a building in Vienna when I got off the Ring, a streetcar that circles the city, on the way to Naschmarkt, a famers' market. A top dome gleamed a golden leaf lattice and I just knew it was Klimt. He did take part in the design, I learned, when I visited the Secession Building. Secessionists, too, were rebels opposing the norm who in 1897 left the Association of Austrian Artists. In the lower floor of the building is Klimt's "Beethoven Frieze," where womanly figures float toward the ceiling round the room signifying a Kiss to the whole world and our yearning for happiness, some say. The Lover supplies us with an enduring touch of love, stabilizing us from one initiation to another.

The power of the Lover is akin to meditation and unification of body, mind, and soul. Not only does the Lover's life energy arise from the depths when creating, the stories and defenses of the smaller selves cannot rule in the studio. When we engage the imagination, an energetic silence permeates the environment. We become mindful, in the moment, without a sense of time. Daily stressors and plans to control have no room to destroy peace when one draws, paints, sits at the potter's wheel. These methods calmed not only my mind but reduced the tension in my body greatly, likely turning off my sympathetic nervous system. For some individuals, art may be compared equally to meditation because grocery lists, chores, and petty grudges cannot pop up during the process, because the activity is so absorbing.

While at first I thought I had to be an artist for a living to be truly myself, I found that to be false. I tried twice to enter a fine arts program but was rejected. Nor am I a superior dancer or golfer. I still don't know who I am. You can describe me as average, although my life path is not ordinary. Essentially, I'm an introverted, bookish, curious, sleuth-like thing, ever seeking mystery, ever uncovering meaning, wanting to help others suffer less by learning self-compassion. I know there is a spiritual, imaginative world available to everyone. Consider, we all have imaginations, we all dream, most of us can reflect. *We don't need to have talent to let art be therapy.*

Self-expression means to gain awareness of emotions; more importantly, the arts touch archetypal patterns present in culture. This is what art movements do. The surrealists, for example, in about 1920, became interested in how to release creativity from the unconscious, likely because Austrian psychoanalyst Sigmund Freud, Jung, and others were exploring the same landscape. Surrealists placed unrelated objects next together and used contradictory light sources to mess with the mind. I painted a mural on my bedroom wall using these techniques, depicting Greek statues and columns near an IV bag hooked up to a plant. People like artists Frida Kahlo, Pablo Picasso, and Salvador Dalí were surrealists. I visited Dalí's museum in Beechwood, Ohio, regularly before it landed next in St. Petersburg, Florida. His melted clocks spoke of the timeless element of the unconscious. How he tapped into the spirit realm was to fall asleep in a chair with a key. When the key dropped, he woke to recall a hypnagogic image, in the twilight time just before falling into deeper sleep. Dalí thought of himself as a mystic; he allowed dream imagery and art to guide him so he could inform culture.

Two projects in a ceramics class helped me understand self-expression more clearly. In the first case it had to do with size. The assignment was to use a slab technique with clay to produce a crystalline rock formation. Rolling a ball of clay through a press or with a roller allows the clay to be cut in flat pieces to construct a three-dimensional piece. Not realizing how the pieces would combine because of lack of experience was part of my result. Yet at any time I could have downsized the monstrosity I devised. The "rock" just barely fit into the kiln after weeks of effort and staying later than other students in the class. The insight came, however, when I made a comment to a friend, "Could I have made this any bigger? I guess this just proves I'm the hero. Do the biggest, best, and hardest." Being an overachieving firstborn, what else would I expect? Because inside I felt so insignificant, I had to overcompensate. With this piece, I could no longer overlook the hero or star role playing me. This discovery came from the depths of my inner world, but it wasn't like I could stop the role just by seeing it. Behavior change was much slower; more messages from the Self were to come.

The final project in the class was to include all clay methods. I decided to make a mask, selecting elements from several masks from a book. At the same time in a psychology class, I learned about the symptoms of depression. Although I could feel sadness, surely I wasn't depressed. The mask, however, said otherwise. Another classmate assisted my understanding. "It looks sad and surprised at the same time," she said. With three witnesses – me, the mask, and my classmate – I could no longer deny I was truly symptomatic. It also looks fearful, like Edvard Munch's famous image, "The Scream." I did not at all intend for these feelings to manifest when making the mask, nor would I have noticed the expression had she not made the comment. In some way, that mask spoke from a place inside that wanted, needed recognition.

Figure 2. "Screaming Mask"

Though I did now understand a little of the self-expressive process, on the other hand, I had no clue what the dreams were trying to say. *Man and His Symbols,* written by Jungian analysts and edited by Jung, was a much easier read than his other works. In it I found many references to dreams I had recorded before I read the book. How could this be? Now this was mysterious and certainly nonrational. Maybe it was synchronicity. Synchronicity is a term Jung coined. It means that events seem connected but no cause for the linkage can be found between inner and outer events. The inner mask spoke from an emotional space I hid from myself. At any rate, it is the idea once the student is ready, the teacher will appear. These experiences, the dreams recorded prior to reading about them, and the process of self-expression, convinced me these universal archetypes have personal relevance to me.

A Freudian way to think about self-expression is by investigating manifest, as well as latent, material. We know, for example, that a still life might contain a bunch of grapes and a basket. The grapes and basket are the manifest content, or what we can objectively observe with vision. The expressive, latent content, however, is more metaphorical. If dark or weak colors are used, and the bunch of grapes show more stems than fruit, the latent content here might be expressing depression. I saw this in a student's piece in a watercolor class. In a drawing class, I also noticed one artist drawing herself small with huge furniture and larger people around her. Did she feel insignificant in her environment somehow, I wondered? I noticed these events even without psychological training. At any rate, the artist cannot control the latent content. What is inside is projected into the art; it shakes our shoulder to wake up to the inner attitude.

Or maybe with the destructive, reconstructive process of art, my digging unearthed a different face. For example, in *Transforming Depression: Healing the Soul Through Creativity,* author David Rosen reports masked depression is a false self, showing the outer world a happy-face mask while on the inside sadness and rage loom. Eventually, he said, the mask cracks open, allowing true affects and emotions to come forth that can be observed by others as well as the sufferer of depression. The depressive urge to destroy the self is a need to eliminate the false self, he points out.[14] Jung calls this false self "the persona," the person we show in public that doesn't usually match the private. My mask, however, said I didn't know what I was feeling. This subject will be discussed more deeply in Chapter 7.

Sometime in my forties, I slowed down enough, focused, and jumped, despite my fear. Three events led me to a new career. First, some months after I began recording dreams, I had a dream about a voice that told me to paint. There wasn't even an image. I had to go on faith. That is when I began to paint again, starting with watercolors. Secondly, I read an article that featured a Vietnam vet with post traumatic stress disorder (PTSD) who had become a sculptor. He said art therapy saved his life. I wondered if art could save mine. The third instance sealed the idea. It was about a child's precognitive drawing, another example of synchronicity.

Gregg Furth, a Jungian analyst, wrote about a male child's drawing. While completing his doctoral research, Furth created art with children suffering from cancer. During this time, a colleague sent a picture via mail for him to interpret with no questions asked. The drawing of the child depicted a red line on one shoulder, an unusual depiction of a nose, and an elongated neck. He was about five years old. In addition, there was the suggestion of wings and a black area in the abdomen. Furth said it looked like the child felt confined and was on the lookout for the next world as a prediction of death. After sending the interpretation to the colleague in the mail, Furth met the child's mother and found the five-year-old child had been diagnosed with retroperitoneal sarcoma (black area in the abdomen), had a port inserted in the shoulder (the red line), a suction tube in his nose (the depiction was not typical for a five-year-old), and a tracheotomy performed on his neck (elongated). The child, he learned, died (feeling of confinement and wings). Even more profoundly, the child drew the image ten months prior to his diagnosis.[15] This eerie report confirmed there is more than meets the eye. I finally listened to what I knew in my bones, opening my inner ears to her nudging. She awakened me to a new profession, art therapy.

So, what is art therapy? Art therapy is a mental health profession used to help people to become more self-aware and to make positive behavior changes. It became a profession in the 1930s and became recognized in the mid-1960s for its role in healing. Art therapy uses art media to allow expression of thoughts, attitudes, and feelings previously hidden often without intention of the artist. No prior art training is needed; the process, not the product, is the focus. There is no right or wrong in creating an image.

Art therapists (AT) are trained in history, theory, counseling theories, diagnostic and assessment methods, interpersonal skills, treatment planning, and facilitation of group and individual therapy in a variety of settings. For example, ATs are employed in spinal cord injury units, nursing homes, hospices, renal care facilities, group homes, schools, convents, partial hospitalization and intensive outpatient treatment centers, and private practices. ATs were required to study research and produce a thesis when I went to graduate school, so they could obtain a master's in art therapy counseling. They also are trained to practice mindful observation of images to ask questions that might be relevant to treatment. The client indicates what the image is about for them. The AT does not interpret. Many ATs acquire supervision and become registered and board certified in art therapy and licensed in counseling.

Art therapy can be from a psychoanalytic perspective or from an art-as-therapy perspective. Many ATs view Jung as the father of art therapy. While I am trained in both, I generally use an art psychotherapy approach using mindfulness.

Art is an effective way to express emotions through color, line, shape, and form, non-verbally. As emotions are pure energy, art can make that energy tangible. Most people react to them by tensing, judging, or denying. With art, however, emotions can be identified and approached in a less threatening manner than use of words. The client can learn to step back from emotions and have more choice about what actions she might take next by using the image. Art can also help physically by showing patterns of tension. Here, the client accepts pain by observing the image, rather than fighting it. Spiritually, art can help us connect with our own wise mind and to make healthy changes. Art therapy is about gaining empowerment and instruction from within with or without words.

Some examples of art therapy images

This image was completed while I was undergoing therapy, showing how my body felt in relation to a dream about being held hostage.

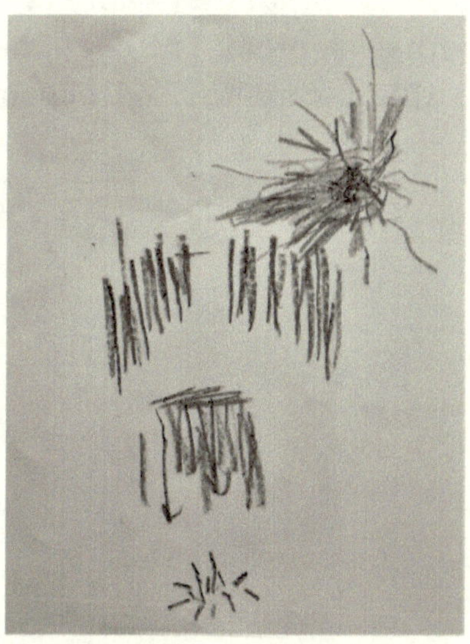

Figure 3. "Hostage Body Tension"

Below is a piece by a patient at a hospice facility who was worried how her adult son could manage once she died. She decorated a cardboard box and put words of encouragement to him on the strips of paper.

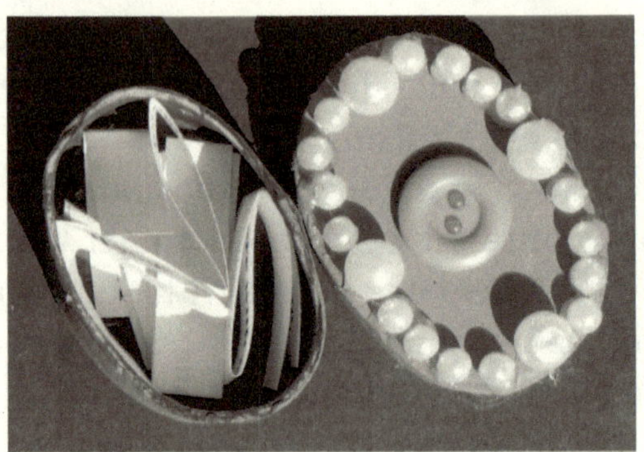

Figure 4. "Reassurance"

Figure 5 was completed in individual therapy. The art intervention was to draw your good self and your bad self. The client then did a dialogue with the images, asking each why they were here and what they wanted. Then the images had a dialogue with each other. The client heard the images be critical. With this awareness, he began to change his negative self-talk.

Figure 5. "Good Self/Bad Self"

CHAPTER 2: THE GATE

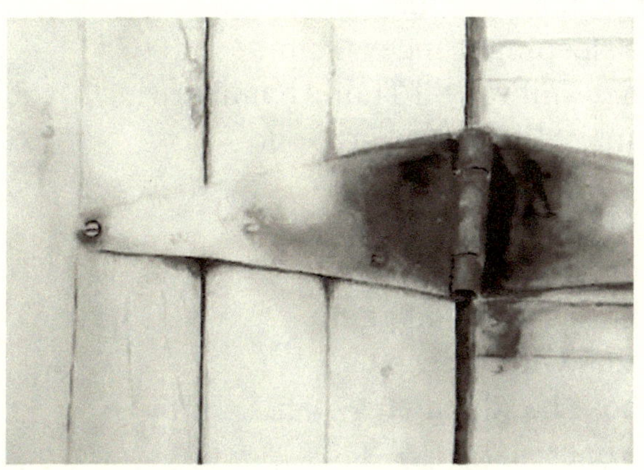

Figure 6. "Gate"

"The Gate: An Opening for Sound"
From what angel's earring
what golden tune
what book we passed
and all consumed
transformed to stones
and placed in my bowel
did i see my sorrow
become the sound?

But Judas hangs my letters
upside down and i fall

from the House of God
to stumble, fall
as Babel's language crumbles
twisted tongues, twisted tongues.

Mute scattered people, we are shards
unable to grasp or hold.
What lightning must inside explode
what vaginal justice, foolish T
what pea will fling
the sleeping princess round?
What timbre will Thor's hammer ring
to mark the sacred ground.

Yet Hers is the Image
I cannot see
Whose childhood pains
Oozed with my plea
Whose hands catch
the babe
emergent from my knee
Tell me, O angel, are you
my delivery?

"Latent"
Silently O nation stir
let your plastic movements design
color, tone, light, and rhyme.
From what region will they shine
picturing
hymn upon hymn, sign upon sign?
Felt yet not seen
for no evidence remains
save for paintings and harmonic waves

save for creatures dancing
prehistoric caves
save for narrow passageways.
From here She calls.
Stone-bound and aching.

What is about to unfold is opening to the imagination, how images are like divine portals. Attending to them is what Rodger Canals calls "visual creativity," a devotion to the Venezuelan goddess Maria Lionza. By creating and contemplating images, we connect to the Self. Talent is not needed. That is, art connects us to the unconscious, so its contents become known. One artform activates creativity in another. Furthermore, the image soothes the artist and assists development by releasing painful feelings and memories.

Object relations theory is a developmental approach to therapy that overlaps the creative process, especially when using self-portraits. When I viewed my creation, by using a mirror, an intangible presence looked back, my wise mind or angel. Just as the infant needs to see its emotions in the mother's face to know and love herself, so does the adult artist if this didn't occur. This progress is illustrated by four, personal images and my personal family tree. As Carl Jung points out, art is active imagination. It opens us.

Inside the gate, an image nation stirs. Sometimes it knocks; sometimes the nation is at war so no decision can be made. Yet I ignored warnings given in dreams and meditations, as if my image nation wasn't real. Given instructions that certain men weren't good for me, I remember saying, "You don't like any of them!" But the images spoke truth. They were precognitive. In one instance, I had a dream my current boyfriend was involved in a ménage à trois.

He slipped up and gave me his ex-wife's number. When I spoke to her, she said he was still married! No matter what I did, the dream images still attempted to help. So, if you feel at a loss and don't know what to do, open yourself to your dreams and take an art class just because. Both are entrances to the inner world and to the beyond. Jung points this out in "Sermo VII": "Man is a gateway, through which from the outer world of gods, daemons, and soul ye pass into the inner world; out of the greater into the smaller world."[16] You are more than what you think. Her language is other than thinking.

In many ways, images are the heart's expression. They enlarge the confining or limited ego-perspective. In sculpture, drawing, and painting, the artist also has to look beyond one point of view. That is because eye level, lighting, distance, and position affect the object being drawn, the painting being painted. It is not only infinitely different with only a slight shift of the artist's head, the object is always different because it is rendered as part of the context with other colors affecting it and with the artist's feelings, which are different on any given day. With the image, the artist touches that mystery of the infinite and the other. During the process of art there is magic going on, a grasping of the vastness of possibilities for beauty, a nudging toward tolerance. We can look down, but we can also look up, go around, distort, or eliminate. The artist who learns to draw somehow learns multiple viewpoints, reducing the effects of personalization and of judgment.

Children understand images long before they understand words. How is it then we might come to understand picture-language? We draw upon it all the time. The mind works with images in a much greater capacity than we are generally aware. Try to remember where you last had a missing object, for example, and an image will arise. Or try to solve a mathematical story problem. You will see in your mind a picture story with a possible solution.

Mnemonic or memory aids additionally involve combinations of letters and pictures to aid recall. Furthermore, images collect about them moods that install a sense of fascination. Look at any child play to glimpse unreserved emotional animation at its best. Some say an image is the play of the gods turning upside down the mundane to reach into the realm of possibility. Images are the stuff and flight of imagination, connecting the disparate, reconnecting the severed, moving cemented forms and stifling conditions in a vivifying vocabulary foreign and dark to commonplace states of being. Further, historian Mircea Eliade writes that the image "unveils aspects of ultimate reality that are otherwise inaccessible."[17]

Pictures, images, and statues seem to invite the energy of the spirit world. For example, Buddhism, shamanism, ceremonial magic, yoga, and Christianity all utilize images. I recall my guru specifically instructing to always have a picture of Buddha or a statue present, even if traveling, when meditating.

Similarly, Tibetan meditation incorporates holding the image of a deity in the mind's eye, as a passage and connection to the beyond. We also have ritual implements like the drum and bell and a secret set of pictures not to be seen by the uninitiated. These were given after a Tantric teaching to the newcomer on the "quick path" to enlightenment.

Figure 7. "Buddha Statue"

Figure 8. "Shaman"[18]

The shaman and shamanka (female shaman) contact the spirits to assist in healing others using art and ritual instruments as above. Secondly, ceremonial magic employs the use of Tarot. When I practiced Christian Kabbalah, for example, I meditated on Tarot images and tried to hold them in my mind's eye after looking at the card. Third, I attended a Yogananda retreat where pictures of the yoga lineage were displayed. Lastly, think of Catholicism with statues and pictures of Mary, Jesus, and saints.

Figure 9. "Tarot Star Card" (Rider-Waite deck)[19]

Art therapists, although not actual shaman, use various rituals like drumming or making sounds related to a painted image to increase the angel's messages. I saw this in a workshop at Ursuline College with art therapist and author Shaun McNiff, PhD. In his weekend workshop, we also painted either a dream or an image that arose during meditation to his drumbeat. One image I recalled making was of a fledgling bird, another involved a snake. Anyway, we acted out the image and used body movement to boost the signal to better hear. The space we created together was sacred. The image was sacred. Similarly, when I was in graduate school, we practiced shaman-like rituals by selecting found objects in a darkened room filled with soft music and then created an assemblage, picture, or sculpture. It was like dipping into the void and landing back on earth. Art therapists hunt symbolic meanings that the art suggests. Joseph Campbell further says the shaman can be likened to a priest. What differs the priest from the shaman in North America is that priests come from planting groups, and shaman from hunters. A shaman/shamanka, he writes, after a "personal psychological crisis" opens himself to spiritual guides and guardians and gains power from them[20]

Figure 10. "Sorrowful Mother Float"

Furthermore, anthropologist and author Roger Canals, writing about the cult of Maria Lionza in Venezuela investigated imagery and ritual during his field work for his PhD. He states that artists, dreamers, mediums, and believers worship Maria Lionza by creating altars, statues, paintings, collages, and comic strips of this divinity. Canals calls this "visual creativity"; that is, the artist creates with Maria Lionza in an act of devotion to her. By touching the statue with affection, a relationship with the goddess is established.[21] Therefore, visual creativity provides a gate, portal, or opening to the archetypes within.

Figure 11. "Estatua de Maria Lionza"[22]

Statues and imagery had importance and sacredness in goddess cultures, prior to the establishment of the patriarchy in about 3500 BC. Mystery, however, was replaced with solar consciousness, logic, and facts. Islam and Protestants banned the graven image, although religious forms retained significance in Catholicism. Still, dream images, too hazy for an exact definition, are generally discarded as unreliable, even meaningless. On the other hand, Jungian author Edward Edinger states the image separates the subject (the ego) from the object (the unconscious). We see it, and this becomes an act of knowing (like gnosis). The mirror symbolizes the "psyche's ability to perceive objectively" and is way to avert our gaze from "the grip of raw, primordial being." Images in art and dreams provide this mirror once we open the gate. Science is simply knowing; the image, however, provides the potential for a "knowing with" the Self.[23]

In my first college drawing class, for example, I understood how to separate from my ego. My instructor said we weren't learning to draw; we were learning to see. This seeing was undoing the simple symbol of a stick figure or pair of eyeglasses so the angle, lighting, shadow, and background could rush in. He taught us contour line drawing first. By not looking at the paper, going along the edges of objects slowly coordinating the pencil with the eye moving along the edge, we loosened up the left brain, so the symbol fell away. Little by little after warming up without looking at all, trusting the process, we could then glance down for five percent of the time to get proportion. While drawing, time stopped. Words stopped. Focusing on just one sense, vision, brought rest as well as recognition of what the object is, not what I thought it was.

To access images, we need not be artists, however. Instead, we can approach the creative life as an experiment. Alice Miller, for example, discarded a need for talent in *Pictures of a Childhood: Sixty-six Watercolors and an Essay*. Like images created in art therapy sessions, Miller utilized spontaneous forms because they allowed gateways to primary emotions better than words. She says, for example, "Five years after I began to paint, I started writing my books which would never have been possible without the inner liberation painting had given me." The images provided entry to early internal representations that two Freudian analyses failed to reach.[24] Like Miller, my images allowed expression of the feelings I had denied.

Similarly, creative skills assist in our development as a person. Yet finding the basis of who we are is not easy. I, however, believe art is authentically from our core. *Anyone can be an artist of his or her own life*. In *The Diaries*, artist Paul Klee speaks from this perspective: "Our heart ... urges us to go deeper, down to the bedrock. What comes of this impulse – however you call it: dream, idea, imagination – is not to be taken seriously until it has been given bodily shape in the work of art, through the creative procedure that is suited to it."[25]

The artist, therefore, unconsciously projects feelings in the visual form based on interactions with the mother as an infant and child, as in Miller's example. This is the root of arrested development. By reflecting on the piece with the help of a therapist or by writing about it, connections can be made to the origin of the feelings. Consequently, art allows the client to rework earlier developmental stages while the images provide a recognition and release of feelings.

Creativity arises even in infancy, according to object relations theory. This therapy was helpful to me in understanding my own healing process with art. Winnicott mentions two terms, the transitional object and mirroring. My drawings served both as transitional objects like a teddy bear and the mirroring my mother was unable to provide.[26] British pediatrician Donald Winnicott says the infant sees himself or herself in the mother's face. The mood or facial expression is what the baby sees. While the mother may not always respond to her child, some babies have an indefinite experience of the still face, "of not getting back what they are giving," therefore "they do not see themselves."[27] In this case, only a Snow White witch mirror remained. Neither infant nor adult can see the self as loveable or as whole.

The image below provided comfort. It was completed in my first drawing class in 1991. I remember looking at it and feeling an attachment to it. It was something beautiful to me that resulted from my effort. The theme of the sea is peaceful. The motions outward in the shadow area are cathartic and soothing to make. Though I didn't know it then, it was a transitional object for me.

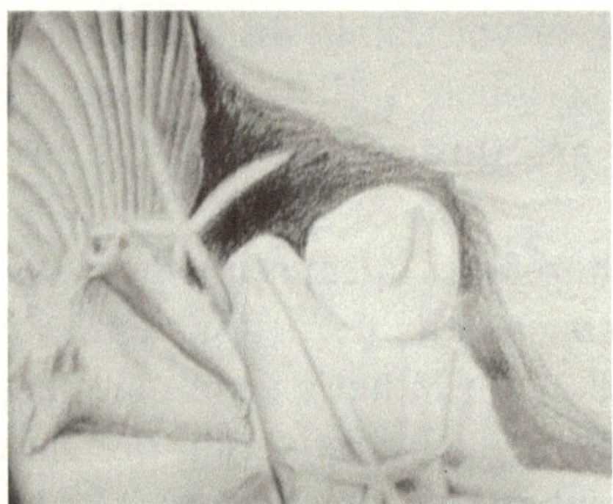

Figure 12. "Comfort"

After completing the following portrait ("Black and White"), I did not see sadness in my eye and anxiety traced in the lines above my nose in the portrait because I didn't recognize facial expressions. I probably had alexithymia, an inability to name or describe feelings. More than likely, my mother was unable to mirror my emotions and may have looked at me with a still face. I asked her before she died to write about her life. She wrote that when I was born, she didn't know what to do with me. Her mother and father moved to another state, and she was all alone except for my sixteen-year-old father. Likely she had postpartum depression. Sometimes a flat expression accompanies it.

Figure 13. "Black and White"

While I may have experienced the still face, images in portraits or dream move the inner world outward to be witnessed and processed instead of being denied. The artist exists in the act of creating even though she didn't as an infant. American psychologist Edward Tronick's still face experiment, on YouTube, shows the infant's heart-wrenching distress of enduring the still face. Maybe the image above displays the origin of my own depression.

The relationship with my father was another story. The following painting made concrete how conflicted, anxious attachment to him was projected on a male model. Likewise, the image said my animus had me all twisted up with faulty opinions. See the writhing upper back, showing a general distrust of men unconsciously influencing me. The position chosen to paint was also a turning away viewpoint significant of a preference for self-comfort rather than engaging in relationship. The model, furthermore, has no head showing. Were men just bodies to me? The images speak.

Figure 14. "Twisted"

I grieved and gained a deeper knowledge through my images; they opened and cleared me. A different image-gate, a family tree or genogram, had similar effects. It was an assignment for my family class in the art therapy program. I was instructed to investigate how cultural problems and behaviors in my Finnish, Irish, and Italian ancestry influenced me. Finns, I learned, tended to be stoic loners who didn't want to bother others with their problems. They tended to drink as a result. My Irish roots offered guilt and drinking from Irish Catholicism, but also poetry and writing. While the Italian side offered warmth and expressiveness, there were also secrets. Entire villages knew husbands had mistresses, but no one in the family uttered a word about it. These and other family patterns affect our self-concept greatly as the residuals of these emotions are passed on to us.

I investigated my family by numerous interviews in person and by calling relatives in Canada, where my grandmother's family lived. After I assembled the image, I saw that I descended from a chain of firstborns maternally and paternally. Firstborns traditionally are achievers, usually overachievers. Many presidents and CEOs are firstborns. Secondly, there was unresolved grief. My maternal grandmother, Sarah, for example, lost her mother at the age of five. When my great-grandfather hired a nanny who later became his wife, Sarah was reportedly filthy dirty and covered with lice. I thought she suffered neglect, likely left alone while my great-grandfather worked at the railroad. In the new marriage, Grandma was not treated warmly by her stepmother. As a result, she isolated; her full siblings likewise were quiet.

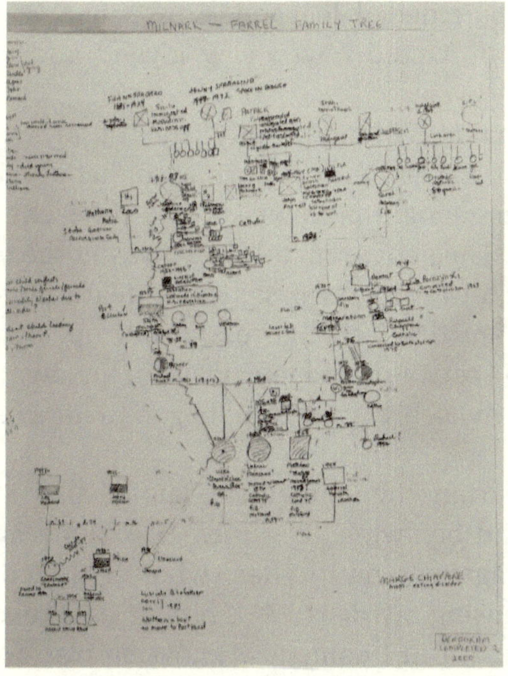

Figure 15. "Milnark-Farrell Genogram"

Grief similarly trickled down the tree from my paternal great-grandmother, Jenny. Jenny suffered the loss of her husband shortly after they immigrated from Sicily to America. She could neither speak English nor cook or clean, coming from a wealthy family. Therefore, many of her eight children went to foster homes. The pattern repeated with my father. When my grandmother, Josephine, divorced, my dad went to a foster home at about age two. She was married three times in an age where divorce was uncommon. My grandmother likely suffered from bipolar disorder. She certainly was dramatic and had to be carried out of my wedding reception. Hints of bipolar disorder went further back in time. On a trip to Sicily, I visited a cousin on my grandmother's side. He showed me my great-great-grandfather's home and said he had been wealthy but lost everything due to gambling. Another great-great-uncle also suicided, I learned. Consequently, both sides of the tree impacted how I saw myself and my view of the world.

I felt ashamed of my family and of myself and was reluctant to share it with my professor, let alone the class. Viewing the genogram, however, is a different awareness than words. The genogram told me I wasn't the only person responsible for my behaviors. Events, deaths, foster homes, alcoholism, and the Great Depression all impacted my family. The patterns repeated in many ways in my own life. Seeing that shifted my self-concept and began to lift a leaden cloak of shame.

Conflicts from my immediate family also affected my emotions and behavior. To survive, I became my mother's champion against my father who criticized us both, probably sensing my distrust of him or as a reaction to my rebelliousness. Did I somehow know he was an unfaithful Italian? A critical voice lived inside me as my father, driving my actions to become perfect. Then maybe the criticism would stop, I must at some level have believed. This is not to say that blaming our parents, although it is convenient, is helpful. The process of forgiving my father is behind me. He was creative as a painter, piano player, and writer. He also became a millionaire with his publishing company. So, I owe him for those traits (although I don't have his entrepreneurial gifts). But looking at what happened within the nuclear family and looking at generational events removed some of my self-blaming. I created the following image with angry letters I wrote to my father. Then I tore them up, burned the edges, and glued the letters inside to the teardrop mandala. I let go of some anger and offered soothing to myself through the image.

Figure 16. "Grief Mandala"

Images enchanted me in yet another way. Although I graduated from the art therapy program, I couldn't find a full-time job to support me, so I resumed a position in my previous career in nuclear medicine. If I couldn't find a job, I thought, at least I can still practice art therapy as a volunteer. As a student, I knew art therapists worked in hospices. So, I found one nearby and took training on how to help the terminally ill and their families. Part of this assistance was about connecting with patients using music, sewing, art, ethnicity, or whatever worked to allow them to express fears or to create something lovely to distract them from pain. Anyway, I felt chained to a job I intensely disliked and decided to draw myself doing art therapy in the main area of the hospice house with patients. Presto! Within a couple of months, I was offered a position as a bereavement coordinator. My supervisor asked me to develop an art therapy program for the terminally ill in addition to working with grieving spouses and families. What a wonderful gift! Was it magic or coincidence? I leave you, the reader, to decide.

In summation, the image opens us using active imagination. Jung described this as "a method of assimilating unconscious contents (dreams, fantasies, etc.) through some form of self-expression."[28] Furthermore, "drawing, painting, writing, sculpture, dance, music, etc. ..." contributes to a transformation of consciousness."[29] First, it releases feeling, as in the black-and-white drawing. I had no intention of showing my sadness. It was just a drawing for a class assignment. Secondly, a reparenting, a tiny bit of self-care instead of just care for others, occurred through mirroring and a transitional object of comfort. Third, the image changes how we see, it bypasses the rational mind and allows an opening to the present moment. This timeless, painless space increases self-compassion, even in the diagram of the family tree. Finally, the image marks our developmental improvements, and opens us to the angel's direction. Gate-vision can also open you.

CHAPTER 3: ART AND THE MOVEMENT OF CONSCIOUSNESS

Not only do dreams and art release suppressed feelings and forward human development; they increase awareness. This chapter explores how the unconscious becomes conscious in a lighting-up process with dreams and art, including my own research data. I describe how repression by thinking causes depression and alexithymia, a lack of words for feelings and sensations in the body. Instead, the body feels pain and a loss of energy. Art as therapy exhibited in clay pieces and paintings calms the body but also marks an initiation, lighting up the darkness when painting or recording a dream familiar. I display a dark, inner character I call Derelict, and I describe my encounter with him in the underworld. Consciousness as feminine, spiritual development is also explored. Thirteen images, one graph, and two poems depict how my psyche became conscious.

"Of Clay"
Fired through must
a brittle shape surrounds
short-circuited spaces
dark signals tripping
gone round and round the crossing
delaying rush hour's anger
to employ witty strategies

or to stab phantoms
on the track that resists:
those vacant locomotions
which lead away from thee.
Inside, the craggy-faced conductor
tells stories of adventure and escape
to the land of milk and millionaires
luring the flocks:
jet-trend-image-Irish-setters
kicked airborne looking down
drenched in diamonds flying
in nothing but red shoes
hollows and graves.
And even if the pot
Is filled and weevil-free,
the baker is starving
for yeast is always

in the next Caddy speeding away.
There is no daily bread.
There is only the sound of mice
rustling trunks and trunks of junk
dusty old crocks
protecting protection
preventing degradation
holding clever plans to outwit fate
but it's too late too late too late.
All is empty.
Nothing.
Nothing to do but break.
Nothing to do but sit and wait.

"Hermes"
By what slippery volume
Does your raucous voice reply?

Where but with your snatching hand
Bejewels my heart to cry.
How but by your trickery
Your garish dress provokes the sigh?
It is time.

Time to crow, Raven.
Time to imbibe cedar leaf tea
To drop the false for light
To fire blue bellicose clowns
Hired for the grand opening
Time to end refrigerated air –
To fly above city streets
Seeking avenues of escape
Time to dance one last chance
Fleeting pleasures bobbing
Down and up up and down
Like a frog belly full of stones
Like Ramon

Hopping through brush-stroked windows
Are green garlanded trees
slithering the heart awake.
When serpents fly
When angels terrify
It is time.

Time for diets and diarrhea
For a sick man
With rolls of fat legs
Sleeping in my room to die.
Time to take up the task
Wire brushing, sanding his peeling
Dead visage to relief.
Time for reluctance and revulsion to pass

To look again from left-hand corners
At dirty rugs and fleas.
Time to clean up to smell the stench
Before opening the door
No joke it is time.

Time to see white vehicles do not laugh
Are not amused
Look different inside
Have no seat for mistakes
Are lost, stolen, or missing
Yet parked in the same space.
When I cannot find
Or be the means of old gold
Or new white lasting powers
Neither here nor there
It is time.

Time to give up shiny new exteriors
Time to heal inside
Time for it to matter
Time the secretary paid
Heed to dreams:
Brother suitors dark and fair
Both ask to dance the swing
One smothers her with wet kisses
The other is quick, light-hearted and gay.
A producer makes a proposal
In the parlor;
A radiologist on the freeway to the sky says,
"Follow me to infinity."
It is time.

As the god of merchants and thieves and the lord of the crossroads, is Hermes asking us to become more conscious? Like the shaman, he is a performer of magic; he asks us to develop and to wonder if consciousness and creativity are strange bedfellows. The following images will attempt to display increased consciousness. Although consciousness is an arduous subject, it includes qualia, perceptions of color, form, and being. Art uses qualia through self-expression. As such, art is an awakener. Moreover, art accesses the unconscious right brain. It helps the artist see the unconscious, sometimes depicting states of emptiness and abandonment, especially in dark man dreams. If these nightmares can be endured, however, they may mark the feminine path to enlightenment.

Creative acts are inexplicable just as consciousness is so difficult to define. Both involve a struggle between mind and matter, wave, and particle. The definition of consciousness is "the quality or state of being aware esp. of something within oneself" and "the state or fact of being conscious of an external object, state, or fact."[30] Author Susan Blackmore agrees that we are aware of something within. She writes that consciousness is being alert to our private experience of sense. Color, form, smell, sound, and taste are known as qualia. These are subjective events describing what something is like, what it is like to be.[31] The author adds that William James, in *The Principles of Psychology,* writes that consciousness includes feelings, desires, thoughts, and volition. Furthermore, theories of consciousness from James onward to the present include the idea that unconscious mental processing governs perception;[32] that is how we interpret the outer object. Neurologist and author

Antonio Damasio, on the other hand, likens consciousness to stage-lit qualia salient in our experience.[33] Many of these descriptions of consciousness consequently involve how art and dreams increase consciousness and initiate selfhood.

Images of thought and feeling are lit up when given outer expression through plastic media. Using the qualia of color, form, and movement when creating, the artist is mindful of a different knowing than the spoken or written word. Perhaps consciousness brings to light suppressed convictions, hidden in the unconscious to be reexamined. As art therapists we see this in client drawings. Core beliefs like "There's something wrong with me," "I'm unlovable," "It's unsafe," or "I'm inadequate," are common with those suffering from depression and anxiety. For example, in Figure 5, "Good Self/ Bad Self," the core belief might be "There's something wrong with me." Since the client drew the image himself, no one told him except his own consciousness. His own core belief came to light.

In a study of eighty-three patients doing group art therapy for my thesis on mandalas, I saw a shift and lighting up of unconsciousness mental processing in the following way. I asked participants to fill in a circle with color before and after an art therapy exercise. The clients drew, collaged, or sculpted images also within a circle as the main intervention. A mandala is a protective, circular enclosure, reducing the anxiety of having to face a blank piece of paper. In the pre-task circles, for example, I found darker colors possibly indicating the client was unconscious of his attitudes or feelings. After the art therapy task, however, the colors in the last circle were lighter. As can be seen below, there was more frequency of black, blue, red, gray, and dark green before the art exercise and more orange, light blue, light green, yellow, and pink afterward.[34] See below:

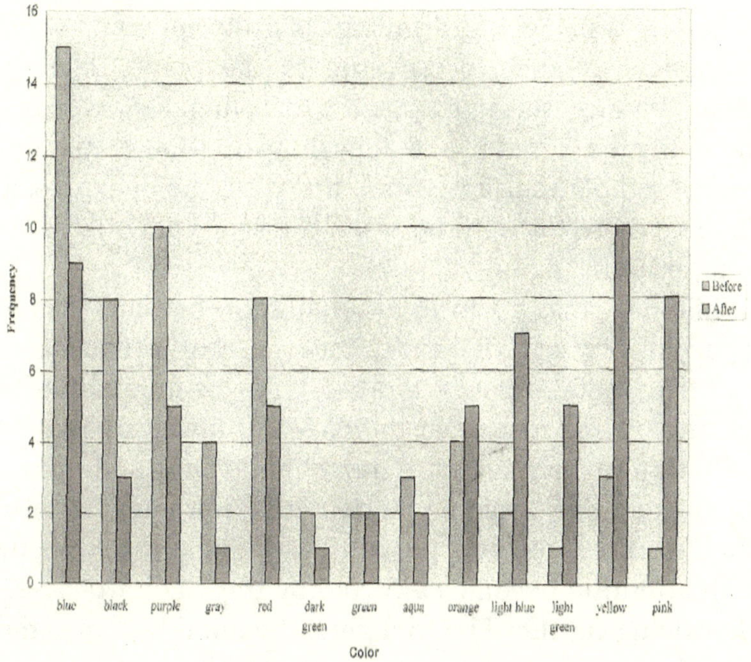

Figure 17. "Color Graph"

Art therapy or art as therapy accesses the inner darkness and expands unity, embodiment, agency, and self-hood. Betty Edwards, in *Drawing on the Artist Within*, believes that illumination can occur from drawing because the left, verbal hemisphere normally dominates consciousness, but by drawing we can access the global, nonlinear mode of processing information in the right. In other words, drawing lights up unconscious neural contents in the right hemisphere and uses a different information processing system than the left. Furthermore, by consciously utilizing the right hemisphere, there is a more unified sense of "I" as a single identity.[35]

In the *Zen of Seeing,* Frederick Franck describes drawing in another way. Seeing/drawing "is a discipline of *pointed mindfulness* as such, persevered to the point where the insight breaks through." Seeing/drawing "is a way of awakening the 'Third Eye,' of focusing attention until it turns into contemplation, and from there to the inexpressible fullness, where the split between the seer and what is seen is obliterated."[36]

While drawing is a form of meditation because it moves the artist out of left-hemispheric, verbal consciousness to unified vision, there are other types of meditation that also attempt to focus the mind. Many forms of Buddhist meditation involve noticing thoughts but not adding more thoughts, so they become stories. It is a practice of letting thoughts come, be, and go without judgment or reaction. When attention becomes directed by the meditator instead of her being captured by thoughts, the mind becomes more focused and observes thoughts rather than identifying with them. The meditator sees, becomes conscious of stories, but does not get caught up in enacting the drama. The meditator is aware that she is aware.

Likewise, self-expression is focusing and silent hearing. I heard the piece talking to me while using a clay coil technique in the following example. First, I began to fashion a piece of pottery intended to become a lamp. As the process developed, the image suggested a female form holding a baby, so I went with it. The head, however, became too heavy and fell to the side. When a head falls to the side, we might think the individual is asleep or unconscious. Another view might be to assume a heavy head is too much thought and not enough body or feeling awareness. At this time, I was mostly in my head, afraid I wouldn't have enough money to survive. The art revealed, uncovered, and lit this up as if on stage.

Antonio Damasio, writing from the perspective of a neurologist studying consciousness in patients suffering brain injury, additionally spoke about the relation of art to consciousness. In *The Feeling of What Happens,* he talks about a woman artist who suffered an injury to her amygdala and, due to this, she couldn't draw fear. The amygdala is a part of the brain that is a threat detector.[37] While my fear and anger detector were intact, I had a similar experience in the inability to paint a positive emotion. See the self-portraits displaying anger and self-depreciation below.

Figure 18. "Angry Self" (1994)

Figure 19. "Fractured Self" (1994)

I don't know what part of my brain was involved, but I couldn't paint happiness. My class assignment was to produce self-portraits showing a range of positive and negative emotions. The negative emotions were not hard for me to paint. But I tried for the longest time to paint the feeling of being happy, of a dancer, or a face, and I could not. Depression and happiness can't share the same canvas. So, I depicted myself off-balance, the fragile ego I was, once again with my head falling to the side.

Figure 20. "Tilted Self" (1994)

Whether consciousness lights up the hidden movements and motives of the right brain or we are dealing with the unconscious in the sense of Jungian unconscious, images and art have a focusing power when we tend them. The power is magical. Maybe we are engaging more left-brain circuits and words with the lighting. But first we need to look at and include all the dark powers that live within us as we make the descent into the dark.

Seeing unconsciousness

So far, we have been talking about what consciousness looks like. Now let us examine what it is not. Damasio writes that when core consciousness is injured in brain damage and coma, there is no ability to generate images or emotion. Emotions can be observed in simple organisms as movements of recoil, as in being attacked, or as in opening to the environment in search of nutrients.[38] In the creative process, we can see the closing down of mental processes of emotion, thinking, and positive memory. It is called *constriction.* Constriction means "to make narrow or draw together, to compress or squeeze, to stultify, stop or cause to falter."[39] See the contrast between Figure 21 and 22. The first is closed and brown as in depression, while the second opens to the environment, as if a garden and its fountain of joy.

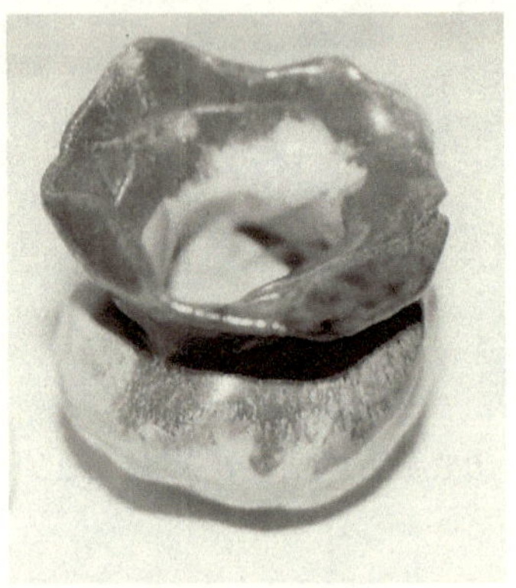

Figure 21. "Pinch Pot" (1993, constriction)

Figure 22. "Mandala" (2000)

Constriction, therefore, arises in created forms. In women's dreams, too, light may also be restricted, expressing lack of consciousness. For example, some of the first images in my dreams were of dark, murderous men who wanted to kill me in various ways. For a time, I dreamt about a figure I called the

Derelict. Not knowing the exact definition of the word, I found it meant "abandoned, especially by owner or occupant: run down; and as lacking a sense of duty: negligent." The second meaning of the word is "something voluntarily abandoned; a ship abandoned on the high seas, or a tract of land left by receding water, and a destitute homeless social misfit."[40]

Here the psychological house's owner does not occupy the body. The ship is abandoned. One is beside oneself. Not following one's duty to oneself, being oneself or accepting one's true self. Fears raised ugly headed faces growling, "What will come next if I am not that? Who will I be if I give up my ego? My beliefs? My parents' ideas? All my obligations to others? What is my particular but previously abandoned duty or purpose?"

Questions somehow lead into some positives despite negative origins. In this condition, I was filled with aversion and dread. Figure 23 was a spontaneous expression of many dreams of this character. I don't recall what the underneath painting was about, but I became frustrated, painted over it, and came up with the image. My angry self was painted in the same manner. Not pretty but certainly expressionist. The idea is that this character wants to be heard and hears all. He tried to drown me. I cry out for help but am pushed down under the water.

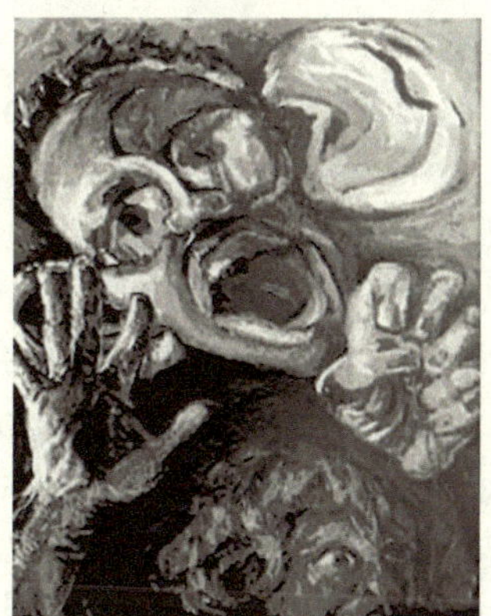

Figure 23. "Derelict"

Derelict might also be associated with the theft of self-awareness in archetypes like the parasite, father complex, animus, tyrant, saturn, senex, Hades, and the devil. Jung says when we are unconscious, we may be possessed by archetypal, primordial images.[41] By an observance of dreams, the activities of these characters become known and we may even separate ourselves from them. In *Women Who Run with the Wolves,* Jungian analyst Clarissa Pinkola Estés, for example, calls this murderous figure the dark man, a predator of the psyche. She adds this experience is initiatory and universal for women showing a way toward increased wisdom and energy.[42] Like the dark man she writes about, in my dreams he tracked, trailed, swooped, assailed, drowned, ordered, or jumped me. Derelict, sometimes a black belt terrorist, stalked me with the intent to strangle. He wanted me to have no air, thus no spirit. At other times, he lurked in dark parking lots or outside my bedroom window. He entered my bedroom accompanied by an uncanny knocking sound. He carried a gun. In one of my more terrifying dream encounters, I am levitated out of bed. I felt as if a Jew in the Holocaust and this was how the Nazis were taking me to the gas chambers. Or he led me into a dark wood, shined a spotlight, and tricked me into following a wrong path.

To tie Derelict up in one tidy bundle of bad was hard to do. He was the force of weight, destruction, and negativity, a mage who used evil powers. At the same time, some parts of him were of utmost benefit because he was representative of the way I treated myself. He is the essence of self-hatred, the inner critic, and judge, the harsh superego, shouting, "You're a misfit, a mistake. You'll never amount to anything! Ha! You're nothing." He murders my voice or steals my innermost needs. These pronouncements twist and sink deep within the gut, where one error is added to another to another and down, down he merrily flushes the emotional toilet. Mine. I blamed myself when someone crossed my boundaries. I thought I existed only for the sake of others to feel needed. This painting seemed to call this to my attention. Derelict's ears were waiting for me to cry out my pain. His loud-roaring mouth haunted me until I eventually listened to his voice so I could find my own.

As I look back, I can see that while I did take steps to release myself from the role of the victim, Derelict's voice still gnawed on inside. His voice usually provoked guilt. I thought, for example, whenever anyone disagreed or disapproved of me that they were right, and I was somehow wrong. The reaction was so automatic I really didn't fully notice it until it went away. I started doing things like telling my friends and even my family no in a sort of "fake it until you make it" mode. I discovered Derelict's voice most fully in the following dream: I've had brain surgery or I'm watching it, I note. I see an image of an unconscious man in a mirror. His head is over to the side and he is propped up on a bed. I'm being taught a technique. I put a vial of vanilla up my nose and up the patient's nose. It acts like smelling salts and wakes me up. I have the feeling of understanding.

In this dream, I am bilocated. I am witness to the force that is within me but not of my head. It affects my thinking. I have too much thinking. It drives shame and guilt. I am awakened by that too-sweet smell of the too-good, of going along with other opinions and needs than my own. When I smell too sweet or am totally agreeable, I cast the Self into the dark. My head, in other words, will be somehow awakened more automatically when I am acting in a too sweet manner. I will be able to see Derelict in the mirror of my mind prior to listening to his voice and listen to my own. Just like creating the coil lamp in ceramics with the head falling to the side, and my self-portrait, "Tilted," maybe I was guided to become a lamp unto myself.

At times, I defeated this familiar after I stopped automatically going along with what others wanted. For example, Derelict was a respiratory therapist/proprietor, keeping all the oxygen to himself until I pushed him down in my childhood woods and tore up his store. As the tables began to turn, I pointed guns at him. Similarly, in another dream I was with a tyrant who was going to make me walk into a garage, nail down the windows, and turn on the car. Derelict had on a bicycle helmet, but somehow I wrested his hammer and hit him until he went face down in a stream. He has appeared with the helmet more than once. What could this possibly mean?

Author and analyst James Hillman provides insight into Derelict regarding the helmet and the underworld environment. He writes that Hades and Hermes wear a cap or helmet that provides invisibility. Hence, we cannot know their hidden intentions, often viewed as terrifying, deceptive, and incalculable but can also contain wisdom.[43] My dreams starring Derelict were unpredictable nightmares, complete with thumping heart. While strangling, drowning, and killing stop the flow of air, it may have another meaning in Tartaros.

In Greek myth, Hillman points out, the Titans ruled as gods prior to the Olympians, headed by Zeus. When Zeus defeated them, they were imprisoned in a dark region called Tartaros. Tartaros can be described as dense air: windy, cold, fluid, and dustlike below the earth, not within it. To Hillman, Tartaros is soul where shades walk upside down with other gods, ancestors, and spirits.[44] Therefore, the vicinity of Hades and his influence in dreams may be about the development of an underworld and mythic perspective where nothing can really be grasped, for the images are shadows, dark and moving yet present in all things. Perhaps the dark man Estés identified is dark because he is invisible. If we attempt to grasp him as an object, he becomes dust. Nonetheless, Hillman points out the shades whisper to us from the images, through metaphor and myth in a language prefaced by "like" or "as if."[45]

Depression is sometimes said to be a loss of soul. We become heavy, sink unto the depths, and feel empty. We don't know who or what we are. At some level we fear looking deeply to see what we have covered over and denied. The condition of the floating Derelict is described in Judith Duerk's book, *Circle of Stones*. Duerk speaks of a woman who was born just before her mother died. Therefore, the woman felt empty, sad, and unable to know a sense of worth. She had no mother's face and eyes to supply it. Without the mirroring, Duerk writes, the infant is unable to form a seed of self. She feels unknown and without hope, abandoned and empty. Here, without the mother, the child becomes insecure and unable to nurture or give comfort to herself. Furthermore, the child feels dirty, ashamed, and guilty, therefore sentenced never to be loved or seen for who she is.[46] I can only wonder if this is what Derelict wanted me to know. Maybe he was taking me down to mourn the loss of the Great Mother Goddess as well as my own, personal mother, so my seed could find root.

As finding root was difficult for my mother, dependent on the male, so it is for me. I think of Dante, a man, and his descent into hell before he finds Beatrice, his Divine Rose, and how I made my own descent. But Christianity has been skeptical about women's power since the patriarchy overthrew the Great Goddess and designated enlightened women as witches not pure enough to lead others. They could purify themselves in isolated cloisters, however, and become saints. Perhaps dreams, poetry, and art can provide a way forward for women to find the confidence to become leaders. Author Carol Christ in *Diving Deep and Surfacing: Women Writers on a Spiritual Quest* says that women undergo three states on the spiritual path. The first is an experience of nothingness related to self-condemnation, victimhood, conditioning, and connections with men. Secondly is an opening to deeper powers of strength and worth and a shedding of convention. Lastly, the woman awakens to the power of being, becomes centered, and casts off the role of the victim.[47] Somewhere I read that the Self will not tolerate victimhood. Perhaps this is the wisdom of Derelict.

The coming of the light

According to the King James version of the Bible, the following begins the book of Genesis: [1] In the beginning God created the heaven and the earth. [2] And the earth was without form, and void; and darkness was upon the face of the deep. ... [5] And God called the light Day, and the darkness he called Night. And the evening and the morning were **the first** day.

For me, the first day is a psychological process, as much as the ungendered godly creative process. I went into the underworld and slowly came up to daylight. Consciousness also seeks the light, the awakening within us. As time went on, I lightened up on myself. Most of my initial paintings were dark and only later became more colorful. In the same sense, the heavy, dark cloud of depression lifted with the use of creativity. I felt physically lighter too. Regard how these pictures may record this:

Figure 24. "Helpless" (1993)

See how the first image is passive, static, and grayed out. In later chapters, the Eve and Soma paintings were also created in 1993 with the browns, grays, and blacks associated with unconsciousness or shadow material. The rest, however, dating from 1997 until about 2004, became lighter, less fearful, and sad, more centered, and powerful. My shadow material appeared as black and red, black, and blue or brown after my earlier colorful self-portraits. Darker colors presented themselves especially when I started painting dream imagery.

Figure 25. "Selves over Time"

In conclusion, the process of becoming a witness to the mirror-like images of the unconscious expands self-awareness. This is fostered by recording and reviewing dream characters and listening to the instruction of the art. Creativity not only tells the artist what the piece needs, but what the artist needs to change. With this lighting up of the darkness, the right brain, unconscious content shifts to the left, verbal hemisphere. This helps unify the artist as she moves this information into the clay, canvas, or paper as art or the written dream. By facing the Derelict figure and enduring the descent into the underworld, the dreamer sees her own victimhood and defeats it. The images honor self-care, self-compassion, and feminine, spiritual growth as a birth of a new, mythic consciousness.

CHAPTER 4: DIGGING BELOW SURFACE CONSCIOUSNESS

Figure 26. "Eve"

"Eve"
In the deeps she shrieks a quaking heart drowning
painting shadows strung on plastic hands
darks that cannot bend or blend

colors like a bull needled, wound in obstinacy.
Here the black one lurks to empty, empty, emptiness
to empty dragging emptiness. And I resist
with wooden muscles, a chemical brain spewing
monuments for the maiden fair to let down her hair.
Yet the recondite puppeteer gesticulates without speech
touches my void with her cup until at last I cry, "No more!"
Queer, fat and membranous her sad slanting eyes
Unblinking, bottomless, contain my all.

When my professor viewed "Eve" (Fig. 26) at a show, he said something like, "Now you are talking!" The following is my own personal process and my own dream. Please be aware I am not equating a black person with the shadow. Nor do I believe when a woman dreams of another woman, shadow is present as some Jungians argue. For me, the shadow is neither good nor bad. Instead it is what is repressed, both positive and negative. Integrating all of the shadow is important. Eve, my feminine ground, who had been repressed, is stepping forward in consciousness.

Whether the shadow archetype or the Great Mother, I can only contemplate. One way to begin is to use associations with the Eve image, such as brown (the color of the painting), dwarfs (because they mine in the brown earth), and the servant figure. Some of these characters, I learned, included the trickster archetype. On the other hand, wise and womanly symbols also expressed themselves in this image. Furthermore, Jung wrote extensively on alchemy, the practice of turning lead into gold. Lead may depict the nigredo stage. According to author Nigel Hamilton, nigredo, or blackening, is first. It is a death and return to primal matter or earth so that regeneration can occur.[48] Let us proceed, now, into the mystery.

Eve resides in the dark, a twilight land, peculiar and wild. She manifests our inner state of spiritual emptiness, screeching. In the painting, the eyes contain infinite sadness, the mouth echoing the feeling with a droop. The left eye is larger than the right, perhaps indicating she sees the feminine way of soul more clearly. Until that time, I refused to drink from her small cup. She wishes to be my servant. She wishes to give of her depths. When the ego has hegemony, however, she disappears into the background, a mere shade of what she could be. Her body, her influence, even her voice is lost and imprisoned. She is even ghostlier than the cold, mouthless person seated in front doing nothing to save her, nothing to know her. Even when we do nothing for her, she waits on us. She waits for her chance to step out of her darkness, out of the closet. She wishes light to open our eyes to her existence. Her face is illuminated. She is beginning to find recognition as I began to understand her language.

This painting spoke to so many meanings, I wonder if it will ever stop. This is the thing with the depths. They go on and on. Whether snake goddess or black Madonna, from wherever she resides, she moved me with a capital *M* into the depths and then into the heights. Unwittingly, I identified with her from a time earlier than I can recall. In her mysterious ways, she led me into mistaken blind alleys and through broken relationships in a life which was really death that I might be again reborn. She was my worst enemy and my greatest ally, my darkest moment and most hidden hope. Within the darkness of her coal-like being, she shines with the cutting brilliance of truth if we would but seek her.

She came to me in the night, both giving and thieving. A trickster. In the dream that prompted this work, my father and I sat consuming brisket steak and vegetables cooked tableside by an African-American waitress. He had ordered something I was not fond of, so I ate the acceptable few bites, gave the rest of my portion to him, and decided to eat the vegetables she was preparing instead. While she sautéed, I left the table to use the bathroom. Upon return, I couldn't believe it. She had eaten all the vegetables and stolen my twenty bucks left on the table to boot! I ripped the money from her, yelling she had no right to the tip! Seated and sullen as I screamed relentlessly, she looked up and stared at me with these horrid, huge, membrane-covered eyes. They had no bottom and were totally blank. If ever I thought how it felt to experience the dark night of the soul, this is how it would look.

On the other hand, she may represent Sophia, earth goddess, the soul of the world, according to psychologist and author Robert Sardello. He states she is related to the grail, and to Parsifal's metamorphosis from ego to what he calls "I." While the "I" links the individual to the soul of the world, it also contains a receptive, fresh love that generates wisdom. This wisdom arrives from the future, through earth and the body by concentrating on the inner activity of soul but not in renunciation of the world. This imaginative activity also, Sardello says, is an awakening of the body where soul and spirit unify through the individual experience of suffering and feeling the destruction of the planet. The development of the "I" Sophia initiates is in love and service within the world and for the world.[49]

Sophia, according to Jean Shinoda Bolen in *Goddesses in Older Women*, is also related to gnosis, or knowing in a subjective rather than and objective sense. This archetype connects the woman with a meaningful life and purpose through intuition. It is a deep knowing felt through the bones, like a sixth sense coming from the wise woman of our interior that connects us to the cosmos and to the divine. She is the call to mysticism, philosophy, to what matters to the woman, to what is essential later in life so that this becomes the focus. Sophia inspires the woman to resist the norms of the patriarchy and to adopt a feminist stance based in her own authentic spirituality so she can be seen and heard rather than diminished.[50]

Jung, too, speaks of Sophia as the transformation of the Shulamite mentioned in the Song of Songs. He likens her to the anima. "'I am black but comely,'" says the Shulamite, maybe sinful but maybe earthy, natural, and fertile, too. She is life, wanting to grow. She doesn't so want to wash off her blackness but to be illuminated from within.[51] See the painting and how the light shines on the right side of her face. The Shulamite, therefore, may indicate that unless we are encouraged to accept ourselves as we are, we cannot shine.

We, being Sophia's children, are all important and all have some mission to carry out regardless of skin color, mental ability, social position, age, or gender. Arriving at a new conclusion cannot be rendered from pure logic, only through the eyes of the irrational. Our too-small human minds have difficulty envisioning below the surface. Life lived as only submission and caretaking is no life at all. Women who deny the need to be taken seriously confirm the meaninglessness of existence. Psychoanalyst Alice Miller emphasizes this point by saying, "We live in a culture that encourages us not to take our own suffering seriously, but rather to make light or even to laugh about it."[52]

Yet recognition of feeling leads to transcendence through it. According to Jung, "Emotion is the chief source of consciousness."[53] Some children are educated about feelings. As I said before, I was not so lucky. Mine seemed to be all lumped together like heavy putty. I saw this happening in my first painting class before the self-portraits were given as assignments. The professor evidently knew primal feelings would find expression or he might have been a masochist. In any case, after a short lecture on expression, his instruction was, "Now paint." Without being given an object to paint, I became extremely anxious. The "painting" turned into a ball of mud. My anger, sadness, and fear were never given verbal labels; they fell below the surface.

As I contemplated color in the painting, I thought brown might represent the earth or the fallen leaves in the ever-turning cycle of nature. Jung felt the first encounter with archetypes was with the anima, the female, chthonic aspect of the soul combined with the male counterpart.[54] As Eve is female, Derelict was male; or maybe Eve is both. Brown or black may signify the original sphere of the goddess who gives life and takes life away. Similarly, the alchemists say, the spirit is imprisoned in matter. This is sometimes symbolized by the dragon or winged serpent and nigredo stage of individuation.[55] There are equivalencies with the dragon and uroboros. While under the influence of the uroboros, or realm of the Great Goddess, as adults we unconsciously enact relationships with others looking for our mother, father, or siblings and are unable to view them as they are.[56]

Dwarfs similarly live in the underworld, mining for treasure. The Seven Dwarfs tried as best they could to protect Snow White. She was not accepted by the cruel stepmother in the psyche that insists we are bad for feeling sadness or anger, so she was made an orphan in a dark wood. The dwarfs, however, gave her a home. Innocent Snow White of the surface nonetheless eats the poisoned apple. She contacts her unconsciousness as she sleeps until the handsome prince gives protection and the kiss of awareness. Stevenson, on the other hand, called the characters of the night, the "little people" or the Muses. He felt they were the source of his creativity. In an essay called, "A Chapter on

Dreams," he says the "little people" work both day and night in some closet of his mind acting out the drama of his life. He says they do "one-half my work for me while I am fast asleep" but "when I am up and about ... [they] have a hand in it even then."[57]

Magic, myth, and fairy tale arrive when we least expect. The image below arrived from a dream of unruly twins. They looked like dwarfs when I sculpted them. On the one hand they listened to me in the dream, and on the other, they ran away and got lost. This is trickster energy. My twins disappeared, maybe into a mine. Norse myths also mention dwarfs, who were craftsmen. In "The Treasures of the Gods," Thor, his wife Sif, and the other Gods of Asgard star in the plot where the theft of Sif's long, golden hair was transformed into a gift. The dwarfs in the underworld forged mighty Thor's hammer, Mjölnir. Of course, Loki, the trickster, had stolen Sif's hair in the first place. He then swindled brother dwarfs into creating treasures, including the hair, at the price of his head. After the completion of the hair and hammer treasures, he also tricked the dwarfs through a technicality to save his head and only had his lips sewn shut.[58]

In dreams I've noticed both dwarfs and dolls, who may also play a trickster role. They seem to mine the environment in general and protect by giving intuition. On one occasion, I was involved with someone who was not nourishing for me. He was alluring but was distracting me from my real work. I was in denial and avoiding the changes I needed to make. I dreamt of a doll that came alive on my entertainment center in my bedroom. On it she dumped over a bowl of water and spread Vaseline all over the place. When I saw the mess, I angrily shouted, "No more!" And I tried to throw her down the long hallway off the bedroom. She mightily clenched my fist so that I had to rip her fingers off to hurl her away.

Figure 27. "Little People"

Apart from dwarfs and dolls, sometimes my shadow people were weak. In another dream I put a black woman in a green plastic box and dragged her to the ER for oxygen. Air is oft a representative of spirit, the breath of life. In addition, I cleaned for a black woman and drew blood from a black girl in the front room of my house. Many sources say that the blood is equivalent to the soul. That's why vampires desire your blood because they want your soul. When I am drawing blood from a dark woman in the front room of my home, perhaps I am drawing from my shadow which is now moving to the foreground.

Caitlin Matthews, however, says Eve, or the black goddess, is black because she is primal. Hers is not a blackness of skin (although she is frequently represented in this way); rather, like Isis, she keeps her glory veiled. "She often takes the appearance of a hag, an aged widow, or a dispossessed woman. Like Kali, she can shock and terrify." Commitment to the black goddess is not to be taken lightly, certainly, for she leads us in many ways that we will find difficult. However, if there is mutual respect between us and her, she will also lead us to the heart of truth and justice.[59] Perhaps it is here that we find the beginning of wisdom within ourselves. If we start with the black goddess or the Kali within, we destroy what no longer serves us, "the all-good, only good mother," as art therapist Pat Allen found while mourning her mother during mask-making.[60]

When I first met Eve, she was the part of me representing the servant symbol. Unconsciously, I adopted the martyr role as a child. Family therapists say the martyr, people pleaser, or caretaker is developed when only certain parts of the child are accepted by the parent. If this painting could speak, it might say something like, "If I am a servant, at least I am useful." Author Michael Misja writes that sensitive children formulate the idea that the only lovable parts are those which help. Becoming the caretaker as a child and watching younger siblings justifies existence. Athletic performance or intellectual achievement serves the same goal. In these cases, the child believes he or she is valued only upon following the rules and upon performance instead of feeling valued for being a unique person. The adult becomes a human doing rather than a human being.[61]

Another way to think about womanly development is to consider Hera in her dark aspect. Arianna Stassinopoulos Huffington writes about her dilemma and ours in *The Gods of Greece.* As the embodiment of martyrdom, Hera appears loyal, but in fact binds Zeus to marriage. She desires to be known for her self-sacrifice rather than a freely given commitment as wife. At the same time, Hera was revered by Greeks because she is capable of transformation. When her identity in her role as wife is pushed aside, she can come to Zeus in fullness instead of need, and her commitment to marriage becomes unconditional. Hera represents all stages of a woman's life from the maiden to the widow. She is the spirit that nurtures, protects, and supports a continuing commitment to the community.[62]

Like Hera's dark, resentful, jealous side does a woman first meet Eve. It is difficult to admit that this is the state of being and outlook one has. It is even more difficult to put a stop to the role of the victim as it takes stage. In my experience, I knew I was drawn in at one point and promptly forgot it in the next relationship. I must have required another painful experience to see my part in the enactment, to bring me deeper into my depths to release those hidden aspects of soul. The enactment could be seen in hindsight but not during. Our dreams give us clues to which powers are at work under the surface, but we must be willing to change on the outer to release the power so it can transform. Therefore, Eve was like an inner therapist, a wise mother, who knew me better than I knew myself.

Whether female or male, "The dead God is the demythologized God, a God disemboweled of emotion, a mental figment without psychic reality," says Hillman.[63] Hillman reflects upon the nature of love and the movement of psyche in our consciousness. Like going into the deep south, he states, "placing God down in the deep will entail a new morality, perhaps. This morality will aim toward the transcendent immanent – that is, the deeply-within which is at the same time beyond."[64] Some today feel this God-presence to be a womanly mediator meeting us first with her blackened face.

The membrane eyes of Eve, or whoever she is, looked like a snake. Goddess mysteries similarly involved the snake. Perhaps she, a snake goddess, wound the pole of the dream-healing god, Asclepius, who was a prototype of Christ. As the kundalini force that lies sleeping before it unwinds up the chakras, she again may move up the pole of the spine toward the masculine spirit. Similarly, Eve listened to the snake and ate the forbidden fruit. Although this story is known as the fall from paradise, it also marks an increase in consciousness in Adam and Eve. These symbols, therefore, a snake and tree or pole, may represent transformation and the union of masculine and feminine energy. The feminine, therefore, in the myths is not excluded.

These investigations of who or what Eve might want or who she is mimicked the dark man or Derelict dreams. Both used terrors to gain attention and were experienced during the same period. Images of water and underground often represent the descent into the unconscious. As we research the images of soul with references to color, as in mining dwarfs, as in the underground, or in literature such as the Old Testament or alchemy, we begin to understand the universality of experience. We become certain about the reality of the unconscious and touch the hems of gods and goddesses. They ask we follow the path of unknowing.

CHAPTER 5: SOMA

Figure 28. "Soma" (1993)

"A Garden of Paradise" by Rumi

Everything you see has its roots in the unseen world.
The forms may change, yet the essence remains the same.

Every wonderful sight will vanish, every sweet word
will fade,
But do not be disheartened,
The source they come from is eternal, growing,
Branching out, giving new life and new joy.
Why do you weep?
The source is within you
And this whole world is springing up from it.

When we see a child abused or orphaned, experiencing one loss after another, we feel some of that loss ourselves. We weep and our heart moves with compassion. But having compassion for ourselves and accepting our suffering is a different story. What we do is the stiff upper lip. We carry on. The following describes the process of accepting suffering with two images and one poem. One dream about the soma myth is explored in-depth along with the myth of Mithra. The color chartreuse seems to indicate the somatization process happening within me; that is, how feelings trapped in the body become pain and feel like disease. By pondering dreams, I excavated vegetative symptoms of depression. Vegetotherapy and art therapy, however, along with other forms of grounding, attend to and release feelings with or without psychiatric medications. The opposites of death and fertility may find balance as a letting go of outer concerns in favor of the inner, spiritual world. Therefore, new seeds can be planted. But in my case, ego sacrifice felt like the story of Job. Soma also points to how these trials may be an offering of service to the Self.

Dreams ask the artist of life to look deeper into body attitudes and processes to restore the mind/body relationship. Sometimes we, like a plant, can grow even in the harshest environments, without water and with too much heat and light. Yet we start below the surface in darkness and grow upward sometimes only with drops of dew. The dream that prompted this image was that I went to visit my daughter in a college town. My youngest son was also there, as if he were going to school. Running around the place was a Mithraic bull, which was a living statuette about the size of a toy poodle. It was not really chasing me, but I felt uncomfortable with it, so my daughter put it away. In the next scene, she held what looked like a green baby with its arms chewed off drinking from a straw something from its head. At closer range, I could see it was a plant filled with liquid like a cactus, but smoother. Taking a sip on it my daughter said: "This is the main drink in India, soma." My son had another statue of some sort, and I buried it so it wouldn't bother me. It was of some divinity. I had no conscious idea of what soma was or its relationship to India before the dream.

While physicians prescribe soma as analgesic for muscle spasm here in America, in India, Soma was a Hindu god. Soma at the same time was a nectar of the gods producing immortality. Vedic hymns say Soma was born in heaven and shot with an arrow as an eagle whose feather fell to earth, becoming the plant. Because soma was an elixir, both gods and demons trick and steal for the drink to become immortal. In one episode, the Gandharvas, who are heavenly musicians, sell soma for Vach, the goddess of speech, writing, and wisdom. Other variants of the myth imply the mutually enhancing quality of relationship between humans and the gods.[65] Today soma as a muscle relaxer produces hallucinations. As such, soma may also stimulate a conversation with the gods.

French historian Alain Daniélou depicts the god Soma from another angle, as the energy of the trans-migrant self. According to Hindu thought, the Cosmic Whole is divided into the Changeless, the Indestructible Person, and the Destructible Person. The Indestructible Person is further sectored into three forms: the inner-impulse, Brahmá, or creativity; the in-dweller, Vishnu, the power in all forms; while the heart, Indra, is the god whom the natural laws emanate. The outer-impulse, however, Agni (fire) is activity in bodies, while the transmigrant-self or Soma, is that consumed by activity, the sacrificed, the seed, the victim. The entire ninth book of the *Rig Veda*, are songs celebrating Soma. As Agni was thought to be the outward breath of the Cosmic Being, Soma was the inward, like inspiration. Like the moon, the dark, blue, and cold, Soma is passive and gentle, recipient. This deity was the fuel of offering.[66]

Though the gods do not eat, they are pleased to see an offering. This offering is the idea of offering one's life to higher purpose. When priests drink the soma sacrifice, their own bodies become the vessel as inner sacrifice is absorbed and they become immortal. Only when humans take definitive action to participate in this cosmic ritual can they become instruments of higher beings; can they voluntarily take on cosmic significance as an equal.[67] When we engage in rituals like dream journals, art, and poetry, likewise we make thank offerings and remembrances to the gods as if drinking soma.

As the other divinity in the dream, I discovered Mithra was the god of the sun, oaths, war, and loyalty to the king worshipped in Persia, today's Iran. The main ceremony of Mithraism was the sacrifice of the bull, probably a remnant of paganism. Mithra is also related to the Indian god Mitra, who unwillingly became part of a ritual to sacrifice the god Soma.[68] Moreover, Mithra, the ancients believed, could penetrate the darkness and the hidden no matter how insignificant the event might be. To include Mithra during Uhura's rise to power, he was invited to become involved in the haoma rite. Here, the initiate drank the juice of a fermented plant, haoma, becoming intoxicated. This inclusion firmly established Mithra in the Persian pantheon. Therefore, with the separation of the dark and the light, many parallels can be drawn with Mithra and Lucifer.[69]

Perhaps the ancients understood Soma as the body/mind/spirit relationship metaphorically expressed in myths. In the same vein, I had an art therapy instructor tell me when he sees chartreuse green in a drawing or painting, it suggests some disease process may be happening. Similarly, disease presents in grief and other psychological disorders if feelings are suppressed. During the time, I thought I suffered lupus or cancer because my energy level was so depleted. My legs felt wooden, like they wouldn't carry me. Most of my body ached, as if I had the flu. Odors and fragrances would start off as a headache, later leaving the feeling that I was unplugged – no more electricity in my body. After many blood tests, the first doctor said, "There's nothing wrong." Following this, I was diagnosed with fibromyalgia by another doctor. She counted sensitive pressure points on my trunk and limbs to arrive at her conclusion. As treatment, I was given an antidepressant sample. I had no idea that my bodily symptoms stemmed from depression.

While this dream and image reflected my physical and emotional state, as I began to express myself in art and poetry, however, I found bodily symptoms abating. One day, for example, I went to the ceramics studio with a cold. I was all achy. But centering the blob of clay and drawing it up on the wheel allowed my symptoms to vanish, even my runny nose! It was so obvious, I decided to write my thesis on the use of mandalas. As the potter's wheel was round, so are mandalas. They also are known to be healing. Focusing and centering, consequently, seemed to release some of the trapped tension in my body as I expressed myself in clay.

When not creating an art form, however, depression nonetheless affected me physically. I also felt sad, hopeless, helpless, guilty, irritable, and I couldn't make decisions.

These are the other components of depression I suffered. As a woman, I was set up for it. Hormones, work and family stressors, and a denigration of feminine power are other factors precursory to depression. As a result, the ratio is that for every man, two women are depressed. Furthermore, I was taught sex and the body were shameful. Christianity has also established strong, unconscious beliefs the body is sinful, bad, and animal-like. A part of me, consequently, felt sinful simply because I was a woman.

Perhaps Soma was a message of changing this attitude, using horror. Most people would be abhorred at the idea a mother had sacrificed and was eating her own child. This is the problem of using the mind in such a superficial way. We look and make a quick assumption and think we are correct. Soma, however, asks that we come closer and have a deeper look into the body of content. How is this image like me? The eaten cactus baby and the buried divinity imply an imagery of death. Or is a part of me drawing upon the wisdom of death because I am drinking from the brains of the baby?

Other dreams in this period similarly echo Soma's garden themes. Plots involved the theft of the seed, my seed, and information about a plant. In one dream, I'm crouching underneath a basement window. I hide because I know something this person wants but I am not about to give it up. No one can see me.

We can look at the seed symbol in a few ways. According to Kabbalah, the "New Plant" is related to an awakening of the inner quest, beginning of course with the seed.[70] In Buddhism is the idea of the karmic seeds we carry that bring forth unwanted events from negative actions in prior lives. Or there is the idea of semen as seed and of the prohibitions of sexuality and sacrifice in the Bible. For example, the proposed murder of Isaac, the fruit of

Abraham's seed, was demanded by Yahweh as a test of faith. These trials, like the Soma rituals, include the acceptance that life is suffering.

The seed metaphor similarly extends to Gnosticism and Jung's procedure for wholeness. For example, according to the gnostic, Valentinian myth, Bythos was a perfect, unbegotten emptiness. Residing with Him was Sige (Silence) and, having an idea to emanate Himself from the serenity, he placed in Sige's womb something like a seed. She thereby became pregnant and issued Nous (Mind) and gave birth to all the other Aeons.[71] Jung, however, relates the seed to the first part of the individuation process. Using Christ as a triune symbol for self-development, Jung writes that individuation consists of three sonships. The first is Christ the Ogdoad, or spirit. The second sonship is Christ the Hebdomad, or soul. The third is the seed and body, Jesus, the son of Mary.[72] The plant in Christianity, however, also can be an extension of fertility myth related to the suffering Christ who like a plant dies but who is resurrected.

This vegetative spirit in alchemy is also thought to be Mercurius (Hermes in Greek myth), the shapeshifter. Imprisoned in matter, Mercurius is freed by angels of the sun and moon who install desires into the wicked, cause terror, and then begin to sweat with fear. This moisture then drops to the earth and becomes fertilization for the plant.[73] Therefore, this also is an image of a seed (Mercurius) planted during the new moon in moist, dark earth and growing up toward the heat and light of the sun. But it is also about the feminine sacrifice of Soma.

My ego, of course, did not want to accept sacrifice. I wanted to be someone and recognized as an artist. But my paintings seemed so ugly! What is it that directed me to art when talent wasn't supplied? No, I focused on the background, the foreground, mixed new colors. Adjusted the bottom, the top. I kept painting even though I was blind, even though the browns and grays seem to bring no harmony, the pinks and greens no spring growth. I dug deeper and again fell into my own grave. Up and down, up and down, I prayed when there was nothing left to pray for. I asked to understand, to find strength but I didn't believe I had any. Not only were dreams and images carrying this extreme tension, so was my outer life. My marriage was failing, my last child was about to leave home, and my hopes for a career in fine arts were over. Yet the conflict fortified my courage and installed self-knowledge. The painting was telling me to pay attention to how my unconscious memories and related feelings were affecting my body.

Wilhelm Reich, an Austrian doctor and psychoanalyst, following the Freudian tradition, believed in somatic treatment for mental conflicts. He wrote and developed a therapy addressing mental difficulties through the mind/body interface by using what he called "functional psychosomatic relationships."[74] Reich practiced Vegetotherapy, a method of dissolving what he called "character armor." This armor included body sensations like muscle tension, sensations of heat and cold, falling, as well as pleasurable sensations of sex. Like the cactus baby, these were vegetative aspects of the body. However, he wrote, "Word language obscures the expressive language of the biological core," the vegetative energy.[75] It follows that the intellect can be used to avoid reality.[76] Picturing, however, goes directly to the source of ill-health in the body, bypassing defenses like intellectualization and rationalization through the use of words.

Emotions link psychological health to physical health as do meanings of the word, soma. Standard definitions are threefold. The first definition relates soma to haoma, a Zoroastrian ritual drink. Similarly, soma is an intoxicating juice from a leafless vine used as an offering to the gods in ancient India. Soma can also be defined as the body of an organism without germ cells or the cell body.[77] This is close to the meaning of the word plasma. Reich says emotion means "moving out" and "protruding," that pleasure moves the protoplasm out of the center of the organism, but anxiety moves the current of biophysical plasma inward. Reich connected such currents with the "orgone" energy or how the bioplasma is charged, as in electrically.[78] Lastly, soma is derived from Sanskrit, originally meaning "he presses out." Consequently, soma is related to the body, energy and expression.

Somatic symptoms and reduced energy also are present in grief. In grief counseling, for example, author J. William Worden, following Bowlby and Lorenz, writes that humans and animals display attachment behavior after the death of their mates. When loss occurs, there is a biological or instinctual aggressive reaction meant to restore the relationship with the missing attachment figure.[79] After the shock phase of grief, one major emotion that surfaces is anger. If the anger is not targeted toward the deceased, retroflected anger results; that is, anger is directed to the self. Beyond rage, Worden says that physical illness is included in grief whether it is death, divorce, or violence.[80] However, it is in the facilitation of grief that art is helpful. The author cites the use of symbols such as pictures, writing letters to the deceased, poetry, journals, drawing, and the making of memory books are techniques to assist in moving through phases of grief.[81]

In *Art Is a Way of Knowing,* Pat Allen says that if grief is not given expression, it will be written in the musculature,[82] in other words, appear as a vegetative symptom. Physical experiences such as a headache, surgery, or a broken bone can generate an image. If pain or illness is made visible in a picture, the body can tell what is needed for a healthier life. By using words to reflect about the image, the pain can provide the artist with choices to modify behavior.[83] She implies that art is a creative way to release grief from the body and to open the gate to play and social bonding rather than the gate of separation distress. In this way the emotions expressed as images allow the body to find balance.

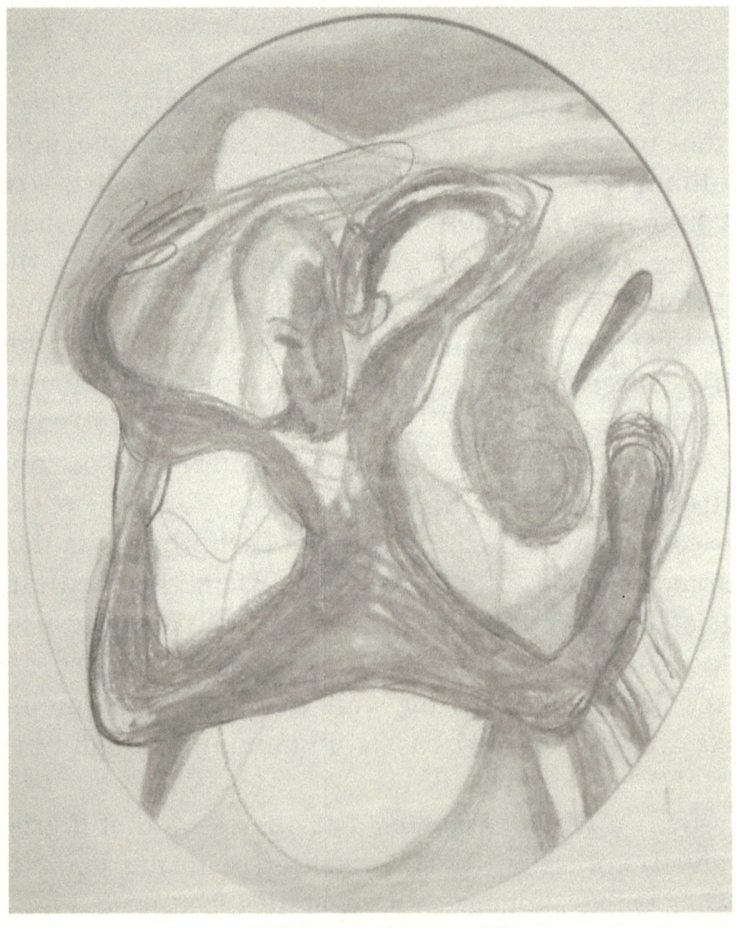

Figure 29. "Floating"

In Soma rituals, perhaps the body becomes like the Grail, a cup or vessel of sacrifice. At this point in time, I was ready to let my old self die. My body wanted me to pay attention and to regulate my emotions in a healthy way. Art therapy assisted with this. Making scribbles after body movement, finding an image, and developing it can bring unconsciousness to awareness. (I will give more information about how to do a scribble drawing in the last chapter.) The additional attention to sensations of the body increases awareness just as it does in somatic therapies like Reich's Vegetotherapy. Deep breathing, dance, grounding, yoga, exercise, massage, somatic experiencing, Eye Movement Desensitization Reprocessing (EMDR), and body scan meditation also bypass words. With trauma, energy is trapped in the body; that is, tensions are held in specific locations just below awareness. These can be released little by little by bringing awareness to discovered areas. Similarly, Figure 29 was completed using body movement prior to and during the scribble drawing. After reflecting, I could see the free-floating anxiety present in my body at the time. I'm not grounded. Note the chartreuse green. I look like I'm falling. Perhaps the rug has been pulled out from under me. Perhaps I need to listen to Soma.

In summation, the soma dream image asks us to accept that life is suffering, the first Noble Truth of the Buddha. Our suffering from unwanted events, negative core beliefs, relational difficulties, or feeling like we don't exist, absurdly draws us closer to the God-image. Jung said that we are possessed by archetypical energies. Regarding the Book of Job, English writer G. K. Chesterton, for example, agrees. He writes that many Christians do not understand the "main idea [of The Book of Job], which is the idea of all men being merely the instrument of a higher power."[84] Edinger echoes

Chesterton in *The Creation of Consciousness*, stating Jung discovered that Yahweh was immoral. God, working with Satan and treating Job as though teasing a dog, sends all manner of punishment (loss of wealth, family, "comforters," physical health) to Job, but he is innocent. Jung describes Yahweh as "the image of a personified brutal force and of an unethical and non-spiritual mind, yet inconstant enough to exhibit traits of kindness and generosity besides a violent power-drive."[85] Yet after hearing God answer his complaints, after seeing God, Job accepts the sacrifices, like Soma, and repents. At the end of the Book of Job, God gives him twice what he had before and Job's friends and family return, offering him solace for the evil God sent, giving him money and one gold ring.[86] Both Jung and Edinger state that man's whole purpose or reason for being is the creation of consciousness and, as this occurs, we come to know and love God so this fearsome being can too become more conscious.[87]

"Soma"
Soma, your Vedic sacrifice is mine
for life is only known by dying
like the wisdom of the leaves
whose voice my desperation stills
as the quiet pond, the flowing river fills
as the breeze, cloud, blue sky or grey
no day is round without its mile
once I stalked the one I thought was me
but Father Time can only smile.

I wait, wait upon the hills
for green direction, for my Soul to arrow
and this barren life I lay to rest:
my hurried pace, my occupations
another spouse, the next vacation.

I now converse with Mother Tree
and plant my garden, water it lovingly.
Like a babe I weep in your healing joy
as I eat and drink the nectar of the season.
Might I find somewhere, somehow a reason.

Soma, body, plant divine
make immortal, grow sublime.
Praise be what I cannot see.
Praise be for you gave your life for me.

CHAPTER 6: THE WASTELAND

Figure 30. "Wasteland"

"Pater"

Breath of fire
You who have opened time in space –
transcendentally distant geometric cogitation
whose all-seeing penetration
burns relentlessly of the order burns
incinerating the humpback desert beast
plodding dry smoking waves
shifting in winded desolation
the beast, loaded, listens
to the trickle almost heard
but only the scythe and rock
seen from empty orbits of bone remain

as the oasis snake dances around the tree
above specks of sand

toiling day to day year to year
money-time in a dusty round
bound to convention's steely hardware parts
vice gripped with screwed eyes
turning unseen mouth moving
fuel in the lost face of humanity
until the cows come home
to the smell of blood
to the city sidewalk heat concrete
without a glimmer of recognition
without a word.

Categorizing dreams, mood, and art under chapter headings during a specific time was like sifting sand particles by size. The following explores desert archetypes like bones and the distant God-image who is dismissive of human suffering. When we believe the universe to be a machine, feelings of despair and meaninglessness arise. The Eye of God is a symbol with other meanings but represented wrath in my case. Yet existentialist philosophy urges Wasteland wanderers to face anxiety using the imagination to develop the courage to be authentic. Jealous gods, however, try to block nonrational knowledge of the hidden God. Creativity, nonetheless, steals it as we become more conscious of the mysteries. Investigations of the male Senex archetype, the bull, and the lion include four paintings, related dreams, and four poems that elucidate initiations on the soul's journey.

Navigating dreams and imagery requires experiences of the dark and wet and the light and dry. In this sequence, light and heat abound. Soma as a cactus announced the shift. I painted the above image before consciously knowing desert archetypes. The image was simply taken from a calendar, yet still the angel spoke. I was, however, conscious of loss, error, anxiety, meaninglessness, despair, and self-condemnation. Large gaps in time occurred where I was without dreams or inspiration. In the desert, we wrestle with the angel of darkness until it produces gnosis, or knowledge of the mysteries.

In *Thus Spake Zarathustra*, for example, German philosopher Friedrich Nietzsche writes the soul must undergo three conditions to transform itself: the camel, the lion, and the child.[88] As the camel, one is in the Wasteland and feels like a beast of burden. Everything is desolate. There is no hope, no water in sight. The anxiety of the existential crisis is no longer denied. Questions about the absurdity of life come to the fore. In the Jewish Kabbalah, the "dryness" is experienced by the mystic along with an encounter with a guardian. Here "boredom, disgust and fear rise up to oppose the awakening of the inner life."[89] I knew I was hungry for something missing, something lost. I felt like a cog in a machine. Poet and artist William Blake expressed this state as Urizen. American born, British poet T. S. Eliot, Jung in the *Red Book,* and others have called it the Wasteland. My version, called "Pater," is described in the poem above.

One philosophy concerned with the meaninglessness felt in the Wasteland and deeply affecting the consciousness of the twentieth century is called existentialism. Existentialist writers feel that widespread technology, mobile families, and the objectification of man through science and reason caused man to lose a sacred connection to everyday life. As a result, life became absurd and empty. The beginnings of existentialism are rooted in a period of intense anxiety due to the world wars and the unleashing of the atomic bomb, which set off strong reactions in great thinkers and artists of this time. Most existentialist philosophers were concerned with the loss of meaning in Western culture, with artistic forms and with religion or its absurdity.[90]

Psychoanalysts and theologians digested existentialist philosophy and included it in the way they approached others in reaction to the medical model of disease Freud posed. One method was called logotherapy, coined by Victor Frankl, a concentration camp survivor. He wrote a highly influential book, *Man's Search for Meaning,* in 1959 and described the process of logotherapy. *Logos* is a Greek word he defined as "meaning." It is a method of locating a will to meaning, the striving for a concrete meaning specific for the individual, a purposeful reason to live. Frankl proposed that human development included man's responsibility to make meaning from suffering by making Logos conscious. With personal freedom, a personal morality or sense of values could emerge.[91] By taking courageous action, we could choose what would be birthed or what would sink into nothingness. Furthermore, Frankl engaged the client's imagination and creativity to transcend, or grow spiritually, to access Logos. Logos was a knowing he called super-meaning or nonrational knowledge.[92] Frankl, therefore, seems to be talking about gnosis and the process of individuation using courage, the imagination, and creativity.

Standing tall and addressing life's vexations in the Wasteland rather than turning away in helplessness develops courage. In Old French, *cuer,* the word for heart means courage.[93] Lutheran theologian Paul Tillich writes that his definition of courage is not the soldier's. Nor is it immersion in the collective. By experiencing anxiety and doubt bravely even when it seems no relation to God is possible, Tillich implores us to locate our purpose and meaning "in spite of" chaos and despair. The Protestant, the person who is the sinner, not the devout or saintly person, is certain he gains forgiveness from God in a personal, felt encounter. This person and "the courage to accept oneself as accepted in spite of being unacceptable" gains confidence.[94]

On the other hand, Rollo May, an American existential psychologist, notes courage is essential in creativity. In *The Courage to Create,* May defines courage as not opposite of despair, not as virtue or value, but as coming from the heart, making all other virtues possible. Only with courage can an individual allow being and becoming. Through commitment to a goal, by making many decisions in the direction of that goal, we use courage. From courage, we find our essence.[95] Similarly, we perceive a certain danger exists with creativity because it causes the gods to be jealous and to do battle with the artist who goes against the commandment of making graven images. Moreover, artists are usually the ones who are a threat to the conforming and risk becoming psychotic. May relates creativity with a longing for immortality. The artist rages against death and continually surrounds herself with chaos so it can be given form.[96]

During the Wasteland, the theme of time recurred, specifically dreams of being watched, about clocks, or a watch. I felt under scrutiny and judgment. I needed to escape. The keeper of time seemed like a "watcher" or guardian. Phoebus, Apollo, or Zeus also may represent this part of God, as the eye of the intellect. At any rate, sky gods see all and are distant and above, not immanent. The eye is very penetrating, misses nothing, and the encounter usually leaves an uncomfortable, loveless feeling. The myths and stories about Apollo bespeak this tendency of the rational burning out the relational as if being watched or criticized.

Apollo was not successful in winning the love of any woman. Arianna Stasinopoulos Huffington says Apollo is detached and dispassionate. He has the "will to power that is cut off from the feminine, from love and intuition" and "has brought about our shriveled-up rationalist order, with its naive belief in the absolute manageability of life and of human beings."[97] Perhaps from Apollo's energy, existentialism was born.

Other dreams following this theme were concerned with the "law." The law of karmic retribution or being born under a certain astrological sign chains the ego to a predestined path, so it is without choice. Yet in one dream we are tampering with government documents by getting a secretary to reverse page numbers, change letters, and turn over pages, and she is handwriting the changes. Therefore, the idea of tricking the law, related to the earlier mentioned Lover archetype, is revealed.

In *Aion*, Jung also speaks of the law and handwriting. He states the Gnostics believed a fiat was given to man by the evil archonic (world governing) powers. This was a corrupted handwriting on the soul, inflicting evil that Christ had come to redeem.[98] Jung called this writing the "chirographum, ... the handwriting of the ordinances against us ... [by] the influences of the various planetary spheres."[99] Furthermore, when Adam and Eve broke the law by theft of the apple, they were not as worried about being disobedient as they were of their nakedness, Harding notes. Instead, the couple became ashamed and guilty when they had been naked prior and not ashamed. By eating the apple, the pair obtained consciousness themselves "so they now had to distinguish good and evil apart from the dictates of the lawgiver." This original sin, the sins of the father, was of our inheritance, Harding writes, not a personal misdeed.[100]

In the remainder of the dream we write poetry on part of the document. Later, we get Andy Griffith to come down a rope from a helicopter and step into a ship. He goes to dinner with us. I had seen a commercial about Andy Griffith singing hymns on an album titled *Precious Memories.* Andy seemed kinder than the "Watcher." Still looking down from the sky,

He is the one we are trying to outwit with the document, fiat, or law. Yet the dream points out that poetry is another way to trick the guardian and bring the hidden to the surface of the water. The abstract order of justice seems to be coming down to a more relational position. Was Logos descending toward the ego with the help of Eros, the lover?

Edward Edinger writes the "archetypal image that carries the clearest symbolic expression of the ego's experience of being the known object is the image of the Eye of God."[101] This is none other than being watched. He suggests the Eye is an unexpected contact with the Self felt as judgment and the wrath of God when He is the ego's opponent. Further initiations, however, move the ego into what Edinger calls, "knowing with," a marriage of Logos and Eros; in other words, a relationship with the Self.[102]

During this time, I also dreamt about hiding and running from a tyrant character. In the last dream I will mention about this subject I write, Jeff (an extroverted friend of my son and something of a bully) found my gold watch on the lawn and wanted four dollars for it. I only offered two. When he wouldn't agree, I went into his house and took something from him as barter, a game or shirt from his closet. Here it is as if I am willing to give over part of myself, but I will not give up all. No, there is a way to trick him. Again, is the theft. Could this be about stealing the light of consciousness represented by the golden watch? "In myths the acquiring of individuality, of personal autonomy, is always represented as a theft, a stealing of something which the gods have reserved for themselves; for to be individual is to be godlike."[103]

Senex

Although I observed archetypes through dreams, a new awareness dawned with Figure 31, the influence of Senex. The idea was to create an abstract piece using wood rather than canvas or paper. It was my first attempt at spontaneous art (I had no visual image to copy). My process started with geometric shapes and the intention to use yellow and pink together. As I painted, the knotholes suggested different forms. What resulted is a window with three and a fourth developing swirl suggesting galaxies. In addition, there are two clocks, a chair, a table, and a tree. The table is set with a glass of electricity to drink and a skull to digest for dinner. The number four is suggested with the square shapes. In many of his writings, Jung equated the number four with wholeness. The square shapes suggest this potential for wholeness, including the polarity of male and female with the round and square shapes. Jung says, "Polarity means a potential, and wherever a potential exists there is the possibility of a current, a flow of events, for the tension of opposites strives for balance."[104] See the glass.

Figure 31. "Saturn"

In *A Blue Fire*, James Hillman discusses Senex. He says God, the father image, and Saturn are names for the senex archetype. Senex means "old" – the old wise man and woman, judge, tyrant, priest, elder, or great king. Many of our images of God are included in the archetype. He is distant from femininity and wifeless, seated, bearded, far away in the geometric, cold cosmos using dry calculations and abstract justice to order an unchangeable universe. Other signs of senex include a rock, a sickle, an old oak tree, clocks, and the skull. While under this influence, we feel the effects of karma, punishment, loneliness, impotence, and depression. These states, however, stimulate libidinal impulses toward the imagination, increasing its function.[105] I painted the image then found the description of senex afterward. Was this synchronicity?

Resurrection

"On the Edge"
There by the river's rushing
that cannot be stilled
in the valley of tears
behind and below
deep in the child's sanctuary
softly, softly as a fawn
I knelt the moss and felt near
where, long ago you were mine.
There, where cows gathered
beneath maples in the lane
as twilight drew them home
there, where grew the vine
and the sun slant in rows
my heartbeat to drums unknown.

Too, I danced in dream
with a dark-haired young man
looking through trees
The Green Man
lifting me down from swings
a gentleman never asking a thing.
You, stolen from my lonely patch,
and I am broken as branches
damming the river in spring
crushed near the yellowed grasses
that once waved along the strand
where I fell and heard
your whisper fade,
as my ear was filled with sand.

Yes, my river dried up.
Deserted Ariadne
waited for the genie
of the bottle to land
to grant her wishes:
lovers, position, gold.
Taking-her-breath-away kisses
are gifts for a bride to hold?
What sour twist, bartender
kills the moment days at a time
where promises are only droppings
ravens leave as they fly?

Where O death-dealing bird
as ashes born of the desert
born of the thigh
is the leaving of certainty behind?
What Jerusalem cook-fire
is the first step toward

the blowing bloom
of your ever-living heart?
The underground bull fleshes
the skeleton in our direction
to waggle his skull
screaming through the masks
where the mystery of dread
wells up through the cracks.

Still in the desert, I'm hunting in another direction, for a star. The dream that inspired this painting was set in or near Jerusalem. I am tending a cookfire with some others out in the desert at night. Travelers approach, and one leads a skeleton cow who casts a glance in my direction and waggles its hoary head. Along with the bones, I see a heart throbbing and pumping inside the ribcage. Both terrified and befriended, aghast and in awe, I feel this bull seems to have singled me out.

Figure 32. "The Bull"

Wanderers in the holy land night-walk the razor's edge of the Great Goddess who gives life and takes it away. She is fearsome and benevolent, knowing with ease how to regenerate those who follow her. In the American Southwest, Clarissa Pinkola Estés says stories abound of bone people who flesh out and bring back life to the dead. We all begin as a bundle of bones lost somewhere in a desert, she says, a dismantled skeleton that lies under the sand. It is our work to recover the parts. It is a painstaking process best done when the shadows are just right, for it takes much looking. La Loba (or Bone Woman) indicates what we are to look for – the indestructible life force, the bones.[106]

The bones and new life go hand in hand. American artist Georgia O'Keeffe apparently thought so, for the skulls she painted either flowered or were taking the place of a man's white organ whose blue jeans flanked it upon a red background. Was she saying that in America the goddess would be resurrected? La Loba? The underground bull sifts through the sand of time, back to the shaman who painted bull images on caves, to the time of Bethlehem (near Jerusalem to the East), to the now in dream. As the feminine principle, the cow is still worshipped today in India. It is considered the nourisher and sustenance of life, the animal mother, tamed to be used for her milk, butter, and cheese, or as meat or a pack creature. Joseph Campbell notes that during basal Neolithic times, 5500–4500 BC, the Great Goddess is seen with the head of a cow, holding a bull-headed child or sitting between the horns or riding on the back of a powerful bull.[107]

The Hindu god Siva, known as the Herdsman, was also connected to cattle and dreams. From the depths of deepest sleep and the soul's immersion with the unknown, the Lord of Creatures, Lord of the Earth, united thought and breath into manifest song. Wandering naked through the forest, Siva, later known as Shiva, brought the arts of music, dance, and dramatics so that civilization could gain his wisdom.[108] Shiva personifies the pain and abandonment soul feels when we deny its power within. Containing and acknowledging this power is fearful because it calls us to destroy something about the personality's orientation. Because the setting is in the Near East, I take this to have influence on my religious view. At this time, I identified as Christian.

Yet James Frazer, a Scottish social anthropologist, so completely dismantled my learned, Christian belief system, I no longer knew what to believe. Writing about the significance of the bull, Frazer explores the myths and annual festivals of Attis and Adonis. They are youthful dying, lover gods married to Cybele and Aphrodite, respectively. The geography in the dream points to Adonis myths at first because he was worshipped in Phoenicia, a region that included Israel (Jerusalem setting) and spread throughout western Asia, Syria, Greece, and Rome. In the festivals, women beat their breasts and cried loudly because the stories say Adonis died after a boar gored him to death the scarlet anemone sprouted from his blood. The day after his death, however, worshippers maintained he rose to heaven. Adonis, Frazer points out, may have been a herdsman prior to being a god of vegetation, as the nomadic life of our ancestors ended in favor of the agrarian. Even today in Sardinia, gardens of Adonis are planted for the midsummer festival of St. John (a Catholic replacement for Adonis), in pots with barley, wheat, or corn.

Attis, however, is probably the older myth, Frazer believes, whose origin is in today's western Turkey. Attis was said to be born from a virgin mother, was described as a herdsman or shepherd, and died either from the attack of a boar or because of him unmanning himself next to a pine tree. Violets were said to rise from the blood of Attis. March 22nd marked in Rome the start of the festival of mourning Attis. The ceremony included taking a cut pine tree wreathed with violets to the grove of

Cybele on the Day of Blood. At this time, priests of Attis, in a frenzy stimulated by trumpets, drums, cymbals, flutes, and dance, slashed their arms to bloody the altar and the sacred tree in honor of the dead god. On this same day novice priests also emasculated themselves in love and service of Cybele. On March 25th, however, a carnival erupted celebrating both the resurrected Attis and salvation for worshippers from the clutches of death. Further, initiates, wanting a closer connection to the god, were drenched in the blood of the bull, slain above them on the area now called the Vatican.[109]

The dying, youthful, and resurrected god resurfaced with the death of Jesus, occurring in Judea probably in AD 30 to 33. Although Jesus was a carpenter by trade, he was also youthful, around the age of thirty when ordered crucified by Pontius Pilate. The Romans hung him on a cross in between two thieves and divided his clothing. When he died, Jesus was placed in a cave covered by a rock. On the third day after burial, he appeared in different places to his followers before ascending to heaven. In other words, he was resurrected from the dead after three days and his death, like those of Adonis and Attis, promised all Christians, salvation. Christians similarly celebrate Easter in the Spring. I was taught Jesus was part of the trinity. The trinity, the Father, Son, and Holy Spirit, comprised the one and only God. Yet there were others. Consequently, the transformation of myths shook my bones severely.

Authors Anne Baring and Jules Cashford search further into the past regarding the bull. They say the bull may also symbolize the emergence of the masculine from the androgynous Great Goddess to later become the son-lover.[110] Instead of the Genesis story of God taking the rib of Adam as he slept to create a woman, we are presented with the reverse image. Similarly, the myths of Attis and Adonis signify the goddess and son-lover pair and his consequent rebirth.

Dionysus, also known as Roman Bacchus or Liber, god of wine, wild nature, ecstasy, and fertility,[111] similarly, was a bull god who died as in earlier goddess myths. The god, sometimes pictured with horns, was related to death and resurrection.[112] Stassinopolous Huffington writes he was the only Olympian god born of a mortal. Therefore, Dionysus hugs death closer than any other Greek god except Hades. The myths say he was twice born out of the flames of death. His is the flame of rapture met by the despair of loss, as in the story of Theseus and Ariadne. In the story, Ariadne falls in love with Theseus and gives him a thread to find his way out of the labyrinth if he promises to marry her. After he heroically conquers the Minotaur (a bull-man), Theseus takes her away from Crete to Naxos and promptly abandons her while she lies sleeping on the beach. Through deep anguish and in some myths, death, she finds her true, immortal love, Dionysus.[113]

My frenzy was more like the furies chasing me. During this time, were dreams of death, mine and other dream characters, but also images of hope in the form of babies, animal babies, lost but protected babies. In one dream, I gave birth to a child from a gash in my knee, a scar from a time I injured it as a child. Also, my body was dissected in a dream. In it, a round stone was removed from my bowel and then put back. Other experiences were of being below the surface, of being exposed nude in front of open windows, of being looked at through the window by helicopters, of interrupted sex, sometimes seen by a voyeur. Men in different characters wanted me and a man from a movie studio asked me to marry him. Whether *Phantom of the Opera*, Jack Dawson from the movie *Titanic*, or Dionysus, these impossible lovers reside in a woman's unconscious; well, at least in mine.

Harding, for example, says women who are animus possessed have a ghostly lover sometimes cast in dreams as airmen. In this case, females typically depreciate men who cannot live up to the ideal, and she is caught drinking the love potion under the animus spell. She projects her ghostly lover from one man to another until he is unable to meet her inner values; she is demoralized and looks again. But if she can become aware of her critical attitude, become more loving and accepting, she can turn the tides and find a real, outer love.[114]

A few days of the flu and the empty nest flew in like a hurricane, as I realized I was no longer going to be anyone's mother after twenty-five years of commitment. All three children were gone. I just was rejected for the second time from a fine arts program and divorced for the third time. This and other roles seemed to be disintegrating at once. I dreamt of death. Of being and feeling like nothing. Of eliminating repeatedly. In one dream, I broke a creamer and watched its handle crack off. Who am I if I am not these things, I cried? A mother? A writer? An artist? My despair ran so deep I felt I was falling into a chasm with no bottom.

In my journal I wrote: "Everywhere I turn there is loss. My son! My son! You are growing up and away from me. I don't know if I can go on without the gentleness of your presence. I don't know who I am if I am not your mother. Not anyone's mother. Not anyone's anything. I have nothing and feel as though I am nothing. I feel like I have nothing to give. Nothing to live for. I hope I'll get a tax return and find I instead get to pay. Pay. Pay. Pay. Own up. Pay for a Mistake. Error. Loss. My job as a nuclear tech feels flat. I start toward a gallery and give up. I start writing and crumble. I don't want to be just a mother or a wife but don't want to be without those roles, either. I feel *so blue*! Help tear the old me asunder that I may be useful for something!"

As I wrestled with myself whether I wanted to live or die, my mind or maybe it was my angel, did produce a reason: to not cause any more pain for my children and to give them hope through my example by whatever ordinary means that might be.

Afterward in a meditation vision, I see a cross with no top, the tau, a symbol St. Francis of Assisi loved. (Much later in time, I visited Assisi and had a dream about poverty and animals. I wonder if the saint's spirit spoke to me in that dream and still lingers there.) By studying the Kabbalah and the meaning of Hebrew letters, I learned tau is the last letter of the Hebrew alphabet and signifies a mark, sign, or signature and in Early Hebrew it looked like two crossed sticks or a *T.*[115] Maybe this was a sign to keep going and that I was being protected even though I didn't know it at the time.

After feeding the camel and attending to the cow, I stumbled upon the lion. This lion raped me in one dream. In another dream I encountered another lion, a mountain lion. The dream I recorded was the following. I'm at a camp, driving in looking for where my friends are, where their tent is, and I see this mountain lion lying down next to the tent. This scares me, and I wonder about camping. Therefore, the theme of camping, like the in dream of the living skeleton bull, repeats. Maybe living, camping out in the desert, isn't a good idea. However, Nietzsche believes at first the soul must traverse the Wasteland and learn to bear its burden to be strong. In the desert, soul feels its loneliness. Next comes the lion, the "I will," which slays the dragon of "Thou-shalt."[116] The lion in this sense is the ferocity used to break up the forces of the conforming to become authentic.

Yet after contact with the lion I felt nauseated with the world's conditions and still powerless to change it. It was a search for value as a feminine identity within a patriarchal world. At first, my viewpoint slanted to an angry feminism, and I saw the world as mad, uncaring, unresponsive.

However, the dream and Figure 33 may be saying, I'm not alone for the goddess of animals is again at hand. In Crete, for example, she is seen in a 1500 BC seal, flanked by two lions, standing atop a mountain.[117] On the mountain top the woman can feel triumphant, powerful, and regal, like the lion queen. Nietzsche adds the lion is necessary: "To create new value - that, even the lion cannot yet accomplish but to create itself freedom for new creating - that can the might of the lion do." The creation of freedom for oneself is a sacred "No" even to duty, "for that, my brothers, the lion is needed."[118] Jung's book, *Mysterium Coniunctionis*, seems to agree with Nietzsche's stages of soul development. The lion represents, he points out, the second stage of metamorphosis after dismemberment by the dragon in alchemy. Mercurius, he adds, inhabits the lion.[119] In my case the lion shattered unconscious assumptions so a more authentic gender identity could be formed.

The lioness doesn't categorically reject everything in society but decides what is right for her. During this period, tents, deserts, mountains, and lions also appeared in other dreams. The desert landscape implied that the man I was involved with didn't promote fertility. I was camping out and not moving. In many dreams, he was with other women, but I didn't again listen to the guidance from dreams or meditations while dating. I was stuck, maybe seized by the father complex or animus and not going forward toward my vocation. I married him. Nonetheless, I was called by the angel to take action that was right for me from a stance of deep knowing even if others look at me as a misfit for being married four times. It's like being nailed to the cross, suffering the questions, "Do I follow my duty (marriage vows) or do I follow what is right for me?" This notion deepened my relationship with soul and is what supports me even if I am alone outwardly.

Figure 33. "Kabbalah Mandala"

The mandala image, therefore, is a summation of dream symbols during this period with a few additions. At the time I was practicing Christian Kabbalah in the Golden Dawn tradition of ceremonial magic. Part of the ritual was to visualize Tarot cards. Look closely and find the Magician card of Tarot inside the tent (Figure 34).

Figure 34. "The Magician" (Waite-Rider deck)[120]

He points up and down, meaning as above, so below. The magician is like Hermes, a mediator between heaven, earth, and the underworld. The archetype reaches further back in time to the Egyptian Thoth. In front of the magician is a pentagram while behind the tent and mountain is the hexagram. Both stars are used in ceremonial magic as talismans or for contacting spiritual energies.[121] The Star card in Tarot, however, displays a naked, kneeling woman with one foot on land and the other in the waters (shown in Chapter 2). She pours water from two jars to the land and to the water. I understand her as the source, the soul, reviving the energies of consciousness (the land) and the unconscious (the water). She has an eight-pointed star above her and seven other stars circling her. The positive meaning of this card when drawn is a time of hope and inspiration. Perhaps the wanderers and even the friends I was trying to find in the skeleton bull and mountain lion dreams were magi, like the magician, following the star to Bethlehem.

Some say the star of Bethlehem was the planet, Venus. But a survey of online hypotheses varies because the timing Jesus's birth is unclear, only guessed at 2–4 BC, because Herod died in 4 BC. Therefore, astrology or astronomy is not of much help. Other theorists say the star of Bethlehem was a conjunction of Venus and Jupiter, or Venus near the star Regulus in the constellation Leo, the lion, or maybe the star Sirius or a comet. In any case, the star and the lion line up here in the mandala, a synchronicity appearing as I write. The symbolic language of dreams seemed to be leading me to a spiritual rebirth. I finally committed to the art therapy program at Ursuline College at this time. I sold my house and, with the proceeds, paid for graduate school. But there still was some distance to travel before more fully appreciating the child's gifts. Below are poems related to the Wasteland experience.

"Shekinah"

You wandered with them in the desert.
They carried You, folded up gray material
a thin veil between the city and the wild
animal and the man.
Seated under the great divide
the Ancient of Ancients
weaves the left with the right
like the corpus callosum
makes two minds one
as the day becomes
pitched under starlight.
Yet under the gray
are ten curtains
of fine twined linen
scarlet, purple and blue
announcing honest connecting hues
where nomads'
canvas and a few poles
call all the Earth home
and neither wind nor rain
lightening nor lions
can harm them.

"Vessel"

Too little too late too soon
A helium clown I flew
Clustered in red and blue balloons
Until Artemis of many breasts metastasized
And ribs no longer clasped what might inspire
For points point not to a head but to left and right.
As I ask: "What's left? What's right?"

I cannot go back nor carry you home
Though I was your bow you must arrow alone.

From your first cry, child,
Upon the mountain your voice
Echoed a golden heart
Wide like on a cloudless day
On a familiar shore
Murmuring wave upon wave
From the glistening sea
From the other dimension
Came you forth to me
And my milk runneth over
Without restraint
Too soon too little too late.

But now in a nest of nails I swoon
As all the corners collect the gloom
Tossing the cobwebs round and round
The greens we once wandered
The laughter we shared,
The doctor, the teacher, the grocer, the tear
The meals, the trails,
The mountains I laundered
All topple as I quake;
Too little too soon too late.

What have I given?
What but osteoporotic bones?
With this the future and nothing more
I send my son and close the door?
So soon? So little? So late?

I pan the kitchen and straighten the chair,
Clear the counter and stack the dish.
The creamer slips and slices the air
No more with handle no more with care.
I step through the fragments
lurch for the broom
And sweep.

CHAPTER 7: HEARING AND HEALING

13 The same day went Jesus out of the house, and sat
by the sea side.
[2] And great multitudes were gathered together unto
him, so that he went into a ship, and sat; and the
whole multitude stood on the shore.
[3] And he spake many things unto them in parables,
saying, Behold, a sower went forth to sow;
[4] And when he sowed, some seeds fell by the wayside,
and the fowls came and devoured them up:
[5] Some fell upon stony places, where they had not
much earth: and forthwith they sprung up, because
they had no deepness of earth:
[6] And when the sun was up, they were scorched; and
because they had no root, they withered away.
[7] And some fell among thorns; and the thorns sprung
up, and choked them:
[8] But other fell into good ground, and brought forth fruit,
some a hundredfold, some sixtyfold, some thirtyfold.
[9] Who hath ears to hear, let him hear.
- Matthew (KJV)

"Rose"
Lady of Flowers
Lady of the Dawn
Grandmother
how I have missed your

gentle ways; the days
of Eden where
you watched over
and all the iris gardens
of the eye
the times you were
at my side for weddings
and eating of the cake
all the fruits
you abundantly supplied
the times you flew
wrapped in your throne
to the great blue beyond
to keep white roses
along the boardwalk
where you strolled
content with your Mate
and sometimes jogged
at eighty
with the snake
to stamp energetic miracles
in our hearts
to gather the quarters
in the dark
marrying
the natural and the wise
the patient and the kind
with the bloom
of ever rising
innocence.

As we create, we learn more deeply and give shape to the entities that inspire us. The angel wants us to change our lives to complete our mission here. Do not be afraid of creating. By trusting the process, hidden knowledge breaks through. We, as artists, are translators and midwives. The stories that follow befriended me to other artists' experience and validated my own. The accounts below are some examples of how art can be healing and how it can nurture feminine growth.

A circle is a circle, just a shape. Or is it more than that? Found in sacred caves of the high Neolithic period, that is 4500–3500 BC, the hunter's art moved from overlapping animals on walls, to geometric marks on pebbles such as the cross, the line, and the circle with a dot in the center.[122] This mark is so ancient and powerful, it could be the first movement of image to the written word, in the eon of the first planters whose domain was the fertile crescent of the Nile, Tigris, and Euphrates rivers. Something entirely new, marked by this shape, the mandala, was bestowed to humanity. The circle has energetic properties even now.

Judith Cornell, for example, used mandalas, a circular form of art, to overcome cancer.[123] In *Mandala: Luminous Symbols for Healing*, a married couple, the Borysenkos, both credit use of the mandala for overcoming a depressed state.[124] The third and fourth stories are taken from *Creative Healing*. Here Michael Samuels, M.D., and Mary Rockwood Lane, R.N., write about their experiences. Samuels notes he left his practice and began photographing nature. The creative process allowed a shift, allowing him to resume the practice of medicine by adding guided imagery and relaxation to his black bag.[125] Lane, on the other hand, suffered from a divorce and physical pain. By painting her body, she reported experiencing her discomfort differently. As a painter, she writes, "I stood in front of the canvas and was for the first time in control."[126] As an artist, she grasped her womanly power.

Lastly, are remarkable effects of art for Elizabeth Layton, known as "Grandma" Layton. Layton's life was full of hardship as well as creativity. For example, she divorced an alcoholic spouse and had to raise five children on her own. Luckily, she found work managing her father's newspaper after his death. She nonetheless was depressed and incurred thirteen electroshock treatments and suffered with depression for thirty-five years. At the age of sixty-eight, after losing one of her sons, she no longer wanted to live. Fortunately, her sister coaxed Layton out of the house to take a drawing class. Not only did she draw contour line drawings as much as twelve hours a day in the fall of 1977, but she also noticed the depression abating after a few months. Contour line drawing is a method of looking at the object being drawn instead of the paper and by going along the edges and not erasing. Using this process, Layton advocated for women and senior citizens in her self-portraits. They were displayed throughout the United States and at the Smithsonian American Art Museum. Because of drawing, Grandma Layton was cured of her depression.[127] Although creativity takes time to ripen, these individuals, like me, found it fruitful. Wise old women have much to teach.

Grandmother

"Tau"
Teapots whistled Grandma
to the kitchen back
where we mixed and baked cake
cut cookies as bells
made three-dimensional smells
whose fragrances rang dinner
called the old man home
from fields we tilled
and turned to stubble
all the childhood rubble

hidden in attic estates
wedge-wood dishes
trunks and animal masks
low oaken chairs
where old women once comfortably sat
removed their shirts
and stitched on wrought iron rings
colors, garments, things
a schoolgirl could not find
feet tied and lost in the rain
until a calendar
deep below photographs curled with time
revealed twelve golden Buddhas
smiling above the dates arm around arm
a Golden Age
where wheels no longer turn the page
and angels walk again upon the plains
earth separate from sky
waters from waters
dry land where only holiness remains.

Like Grandma Layton, grandmothers peopled my nightscapes. Grandmother came and went often by the name of Rose in my dreams. Perhaps because my grandmother played a large part of raising me, she was like a flower to me. Grandma had a rose garden. I can remember picking beetles off the plants and dusting them. She also let me help tend the irises. Moreover, she taught me other things, like baking snickerdoodles and a multitude of Christmas cookies. She died in 1993 but nonetheless seemed to visit me as Rose, a presence in my soul.

My childhood small-*t* traumas locked me into something like a vortex. This means that events like an original trauma pulled me into a state of distress, helplessness, and dissociation. I called it going down the emotional toilet. An event might be like an accusation from a spouse that was untrue. While small-*t* traumas accumulate, large-*T* traumas are more like rape, what soldiers experience in war, or a near-death motor vehicle accident.

In either case, post traumatic stress disorder may develop. For example, small-*t* traumas might include having a depressed mother, an alcoholic, critical father, and being left alone at age six. As a result, I was self-critical, cold toward myself, and reacted to others with limited options.

The wise old woman, Rose, however, helped me move. Vortices not only pull us downward into traumatic overwhelm; they can move us in the opposite direction. While senex means old man and woman and can be related to death, this force can also endow us with wisdom if we can hear the angel's message. When painting the image below, I felt as if in the heart of darkness. The blue fire burned in me for years as depression. I, under the stars, was alone yet not alone with the Ancient of Ancients.

The dream of 1994 was as follows: I was a grandma, a Mary Poppins type, in an old-fashioned, buttoned-to-the-neck black dress and high-buttoned black boots in the environ of Marymount Hospital. This was my workplace at the time, so I dropped in to see a friend (whose name was Rose). Here we have a grandmother with the dress, and Mary (Poppins, Marymount), a younger version, both announcing themselves in the dream. While there, I snuck into my workplace and saw three winter coats hanging on a rack. Next, I took them into this horseless carriage, a design with long wooden rails, like a sulky to fit into a harness. Somehow, I flew the horseless carriage to a street like Murray Hill. I felt distinct movement as this happened. The carriage eventually wafted back down to the ground before I awoke.

Figure 35. "Whirlwind"

Murray Hill is a place not far from my residence where the Feast of the Assumption is held yearly. On August 15th, Catholics celebrate Mary's ascension to Heaven complete with her body. Murray Hill, therefore, represents a spiritual place of womanly energy. Not only that, but it is also sprinkled with art galleries, restaurants, and garlic. I almost joined a gallery there but gave up the notion. Called Little Italy, it has an old-world flavor. The funnel in the painting hovers above the area. The wheel of the sulky is on the right side, and the rails enfolded on the left. Why I created a tornado remains a puzzle; it was simply a way to capture the essence of the dream. When we amplify from the dream image to the artwork, strange things begin to happen.

Figure 35 seems to be indicating art and my Italian ancestry are cooking up nourishment for me on high places. Yet the driver looks rigid and covered with coats, entwined by them as if frozen. She also looks distant, not unlike descriptions of Saturn, likely the senex force again, but this time more like a mediator outside time. Recall the relationship between Kronos, Father Time, and Saturn. As importantly, grandmother looks like my grandfather, a facet I didn't recognize until after the painting was completed.

The figure is a hermaphrodite, of both sexes. Quispel, a friend of Jung's, points out that according to the Gnostics, this image could represent the Metropator, mother-father, or wife of God. She represented female wholeness symbolically. Coptic writings from the school of Valentinus about her were discovered in the Nag Hammadi find in Egypt around 1945. Although Coptic to Greek translations were often mistaken, "This extremely profound imagery is completely obscured by the unspeakable translation: 'Grandfather' ('Grannie is now in heaven')."[128]

This is the second image of a hermaphrodite and a continuation of the idea of theft. She stole coats from the hospital. Does this theft indicate an increase in consciousness? My Eve image also appears just as male as female. Does divinity arrive first as an undifferentiated being of both sexes, I wonder? Or is it our task to funnel the deep and wild feminine to the surface so as a woman, we can be endowed with her knowing? She wants to live but if we forget her, she will surge forth once again.

In *Answer to Job* Jung writes, "only in the last days will the vision of the sun-woman be fulfilled. In recognition of this truth, and evidently inspired by the workings of the Holy Ghost, the Pope has recently announced the dogma of the *Assumptio Mariae,* very much to the astonishment of all rationalists. Mary as the bride is united with the son in the heavenly bridal-chamber, and, as Sophia, with the Godhead."[129]

Maybe our personal myth is to include Sophia, the goddess, or the Holy Ghost as feminine to announce a new era, as Jung suggested. Herstory as much as history. A story of relation, including the male instead of making it evil, like the feminine. My dreams certainly included male energies like Dionysus, Apollo, Hermes, and light- and dark-haired brothers as well as the dark persecutor, Derelict. At any rate, here the theme of wisdom displays grandmother and grandfather as unified.

This dream, one of my richest, echoes an earlier era with clothing, the horseless carriage, Little Italy, Grandma, and now, Grandpa. Grampa Jack didn't fly but he too was outside time in a sense. He was born in Kansas, the origin of Dorothy's tornado in *The Wizard of Oz*. After the Great Depression, he moved to Cleveland, Ohio, looking for work. At a dance he met my grandmother, Sarah from Ontario, Canada. She was employed as a nanny. Grandpa was a very unusual person, although as a Fuller Brush salesman, he seemed ordinary. He didn't talk much about his family but did tell me he rejected the Catholicism his Irish family followed. Instead, he chose yoga, became a vegetarian, and meditated, unheard of practices during the 1940s and 1950s. I remember him asking me to be quiet while he meditated once and, after opening his eyes, I said, "What happened, Grandpa?" He said he talked to people. Maybe he was practicing active imagination, mentoring me even then.

His uniqueness extended to his economic beliefs. After the depression, Grandpa joined an organization called "Direct Credits Society." Based in Detroit, this group was founded on an economic theory devised by a man called Alfred Lawson, who started his career, of all things, in baseball. Lawson in the 1920s was influential in aviation and then wrote several books, including *Direct Credits for Everybody.* Lawson also devised his own philosophy, religion, and system of physics (almost equal to Einstein's). Furthermore, he believed in abolishing the banks and gold but still using paper currency. He added that the government would be the issuer of loans, not banks. As part of "Lawsonomy," guaranteed income would establish his humanitarian goals of everyone having as much as another.[130]

The wheel of time turned almost a hundred years to have Lawsonomy resurface in the Bernie Sanders movement. Like Grandpa being outside time, so the deep blue night of dreams led me to a new position in my inner cosmos. Perhaps I was given the art of the second attention, a revolt from conditioning and the superego. Deepak Chopra says the first attention deals with only the immediate demand using the senses. The second attention, however, is a looking at life from another vantage point.[131] In *The Four Agreements,* Ruiz writes that the Toltecs, also shaman and seers in the dark, similarly believe in the second attention. It helps us use focus to transform our dream of hell to a dream of heaven on earth.[132]

The whirlwind has other implications than bringing history forward, the idea there is nothing new under the sun or as a focusing power. It may signify archetypes breaking through. It suggests a flow of energy and an opening created by divine wind and mind. I recall a dream that was about a business grand opening. A clown, with a devilish grin, was hired for it, and I, on roller skates, circled him. Out of control, I mowed others down. As part of my contemplation, I painted the clown. He was red and blue with a torso surrounded by balloons and flying, tied to me. In *A Blue Fire: Selected Writings by James Hillman,* the author describes puer precisely looking like the image

I just described. Again, I painted the image first then found references to my image in a book. Uncanny. Oh no! An inflated Peter Pan, none other than an image of pride, swelling up on the canvas. Not a pretty picture of myself. Valuing the intellectual and looking down on those less bookish cut me off from others. I was just too frantic. Not a loving attitude at all. Still, the dream was a portal to self-knowledge (unfortunately, I didn't photograph the discarded painting). How could I change what I didn't know? Attention to my wrongdoings wasn't pointed out by others but from the unconscious. These openings are windows to the inner vastness.

Was this inner mind breaking through so I could experience it? Jung says that Nous generates the world and "produces a whirlpool in chaos and thus brings the separation of ether and air."[133] The word *Nous* means "mind" in Gnosticism.[134] The cosmology of the gnostics had systems naming emanations of God. *Nous* means "mind, reason, as an intelligent purposive principle of the world," considered by Neoplatonists to be "the first emanation of God."[135] Was this hidden mind displaying what others knew but I hid from myself? Maybe this was a threshold, a visitation from Hekate, showing truth. It is a place where the wise old woman appears along with the forces of Saturn, where depression and denial can be converted to rising hope, going past only the material. I wrote poems located at the end of this chapter well before I understood the significance of the internal changes. Grandmother's wisdom instilled another viewpoint so I could come back to myself with fresh eyes.

The child

Grandmother, therefore, led me back to the child, who for most of my life was elusive. It felt unacceptable, unlovable, shamed, and sinful, which is woman's fate from the time of Eve. However, Nietzsche said, the child is innocence and forgetting, a new beginning, a "holy Yea. Aye, for the game of creating, my brethren, there is needed a holy Yea unto life; *its own* will, willeth now the spirit; *his own* world winneth the world's outcast."[136]

Our bravery draws the light of self-acceptance and hope despite all failures. Feelings of inner warmth and rescue emerged in dreams little by little. By honoring feelings with curiosity, the child was contacted and vitalized. Rather than staying in immature innocence, like Peter Pan, the soul can move us through experience toward wisdom. This is the choice to consider opposites, to transcend them and to walk the middle path. Male, then female. Old then young.

As I said earlier, dreams of the child have arisen many times in my journal. Her first appearance displayed my attitude about her. She was in a dream I painted, depicted as a muddy discard, a baby dead in a sink, grasping a pencil (also unphotographed). Maybe the idea of throwing out the baby with the bathwater. Following this theme were dreams where she was cold, wet, or fed substances causing illness. For so long, I refused to let her play or be as I obsessively worked to escape my feelings. I simply couldn't hear her in my direness for perfection.

Hillman says the child archetype includes titles like "the Hero, the Divine Child, the figures of Eros, the King's Son, the Son of the Great Mother, the Psycho-pompos, Mercury-Hermes, Trickster, and the Messiah." He describes these figures as "narcissistic, inspired, effeminate, phallic, inquisitive, inventive, pensive, passive, fiery, and capricious."[137] The child not only shows us our goodness but also our tendencies to feel superior to others and to not follow through making ideas, actions. When we are not capable of sound judgment because we can't see the big picture, the child becomes the jester and laughs when the ego takes hold, thinking it has the divine power to judge or to heal. But the child can also suggest new energy infusing tired, old life.

Jungian analyst and author M. Esther Harding, in *The I and the Not-I: A Study in the Development of Consciousness*, observes that while the child archetype can be about helplessness and dependence, it also can be about a birth from the sacred marriage, the union of animus and anima in alchemy. If the latter is the case, the importance of the child is essential in spiritual growth. As Jesus said to his disciples, that unless they became like little children, they could not enter the kingdom (Matt.: 18:3). That is, the individual becoming childlike, full of wonder, curiosity, playfulness, experimentation, and openness to the new suggests that playing with art materials and dream images invites the child archetype. As Harding points out, the dreamer is "touching an untrammeled and free creative spirit arising from the depths" to cast aside habit and known ideas, to become whole.[138]

Ritual, ceremony, active imagination, art, poetry, and dream are all playgrounds where exact definitions are suspended, where one image overlaps the other. Art therapy opens this sacred space where images don't have to make sense. Instead we can play with and honor them. The image below was about a dream I had during graduate school. We were learning about active imagination, the method Jung utilized for himself, his pupils and his clients. The following dialogue depicts one way we might engage playfully with active imagination.

My dream was set in the home of a wealthy and well-known cardiac surgeon I visited when a friend was house-sitting. The couple was having a party, and I was like a nanny caring for this cute, blonde girl who was three or four. We were sitting in the kitchen, and the cardiologist looked at me with a penetrating stare through an opening that reminded me of a knothole in a door. I felt uncomfortable and understood this look to mean to feed the child. I picked her up and gave her chicken tenders.

Figure 36. "Child"

In a class assignment, I held a dialogue with the images, an "as if" they were characters in a play. Out loud I asked each part of the picture what it wanted and let it answer. I wrote the following messages down. The child (I painted a picture of me at about the age of two) being central, was the first image I addressed. She said, "Give me the things I need. I want you to protect me and say how I feel. Love me." I asked, "Can you feel my love?" She said, "Yes." The heart (I drew this because I was in the house of the cardiologist, or heart doctor) went into more depth. "I want relationship. I'm close to the child but not the same. The child's needs are more an internal affair. The relation is between the ego and inner child and the body's physical needs and fulfilling them. Mine is more about trusting others and having the ability to relate in that manner. It's also about repair – heart surgery – clearing the blocks."

Next the eye spoke up. "I am penetrating into your soul. This feels uncomfortable to you. You are afraid to be seen so deeply. But behind the door is your light. I'm like your third eye. By caring for the child, you can begin to care for others. My eye is the eye of unity. If you remember my gaze and what I ask you to do, you will feel whole."

The sun was the next character to have its say. "The heart and door are before the child. So is the hand, your hand. I am behind all symbols. I am the vitality you will gain from paying attention to these connections. You wonder why I am orange. I am the creative power of the second chakra. Its light is being purified. You are honoring others and learning the importance of asking for your needs to be met." The hand, however, stated: "I want contact and identity. I want to feel I can shape your environment." The hand was then silent.

Afterward, the chicken tenders, not to be ignored, related the following: "We want you to build courage and have tenderness for yourself, to know you can digest being strong and gentle together. These concepts are not opposed. The move toward the child, like the black lines, helps release negative thoughts and beliefs you or the child entertain."

Fish

The child archetype exercise was completed in 2001 in the winter session before I graduated with a master's degree in art therapy. Along with child imagery, there were also an abundance of fish and water. While water suggests purification, our emotional state and the unconscious, the fish symbol has other meanings related to the Child and to Christ. Christ, for Jung, was a symbol of the Self. Below are three images I recorded from dreams or that arose from spontaneous drawings:

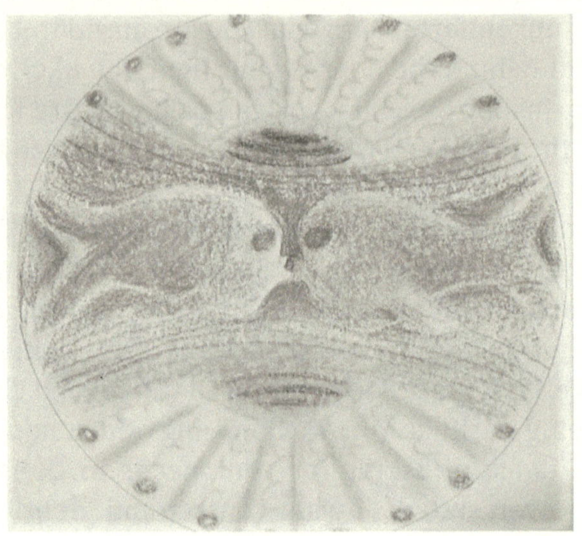

Figure 37. "Pisces Rotated"

Figure 38. "Future Goldfish"

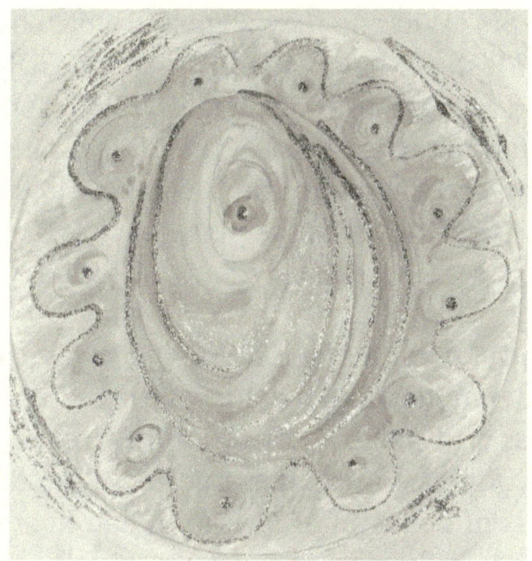

Figure 39. "Round Fish"

Look closely at the above images, how the color, orientations, and the environment change. The sign of Pisces generally depicts two fish swimming in opposite Directions, but in the first image, they face one another, perhaps bringing opposites together. See how one fish is darker and the other lighter and they are red, like fire (opposites of fire and water, dark and light). Jung writes about a first-century BC Egyptian zodiac image that depicts the fishes facing the same way as in the middle image. The same picture has the fish in some type enclosure, like a pond, and followers of Christ were baptized in in a fish pond.[139] The round fish according to alchemy has a "fatness" that, when cooked slowly over fire, begins to shine and later in the process becomes an eyewash for the philosopher who then understands hidden knowledge. Similarly, the round fish has references to guidance.[140] Notice the glitter on the round fish whereas the other two images are colorful but flat. Jung says that by contemplating the images we are drawn into mystery. What do they mean? Where do they come from? What do they want and what shall we do to honor them? Fish are below the surface, not easily known or seen, like the archetypes. The images are our food; they are like mana. In a miracle, Christ in the Bible multiplied fishes and loaves to feed the multitude. Snag them and you will be nourished by far more than the physical.

Grace

Depression sometimes feels like being in hell, caught in the state of condemnation and meaninglessness, separated from our goodness and positive affect. Initial dreams, according to Jung, may forecast one's life trajectory. The first dream I recorded was of being an American Indian floating inside a hollowed log in a flowing river. Was my earthly body in the Nile, like Osiris, killed by Seth, and put in a wooden coffin? Or was the tree goddess, Artemis, protecting me? At any rate, people were shooting at me from above on the banks. The log hid me, but then I went over rapids and was washed out. I feared I would drown, as my heart thumped wildly. To my astonishment, I floated gently to the shore. As I look back, perhaps the energy of the imagination, perhaps the angel, guided me even though my depression lasted more than twenty-five years. When we look and look deeply, daringly, despite the eerie scenes, we may find a calling card for grace.

Like Grandma Layton, I noticed longer and longer periods of happiness, especially occurring when I spent time in nature or with art. By this time, my image portfolio was quite full. One day after I had completed my art therapy degree, I was biking in the woods and realized for the first time I liked myself. It was as if I were forgiven despite my wrongdoings. Nature was a place that I could always turn for hope and comfort. I could do this alone, like with art, and it was always available. It was a gorgeous day. Although I still at times feel guilt, shame never became my prison guard again. This is not to say embarrassment doesn't come and go as it does in most humans. Neither does it mean the angel doesn't continue to whisper through the images how I should be ashamed so I can change my behavior or attitude. I simply no longer have the urge to condemn myself for mistakes of the past. Perhaps the images allowed me to step back from negative beliefs and negative emotions so I could begin to heal.

The feeling was like a voice whispering that I was accepted by a something greater or other than myself, a not-I, something unseen. My child helped me with the forgetting of my mistakenness and allowed a new attitude to be born within me. I felt kinder and nearer to myself. I met the dark forces within me. By giving them forms, I accepted the reality of their presence and left them and the related feelings on the canvas. They influenced me, marking the succession of my initiations from the state of infant dependency to a maturing adulthood. These encounters allowed me to develop. They live in my soul and in all our souls. By embracing them, by being curious and loving toward them, I embraced that I was part of everyone yet a person experiencing my soul and outer life distinctly. Self-acceptance started growing and to this day continues to grow through my images and then to flower through contemplation of them.

Figure 40. "The Three Graces"

While the courage to be empowers us, the courage to create is the "yes" response of the child, an ability to be spontaneous and to become involved meaningfully with one's authentic forms. Tillich says man desires to actualize his potential as a microcosm of the universe. "In the visual arts nature is drawn into the human sphere and man is posited in nature, and both are shown in their ultimate possibilities of beauty."[141] If we think of nature as the unconscious, Tillich is pointing to Jung's concept of individuation. Jung felt our duty was to differentiate from the unconscious and the sameness of others.

We can only wonder if the child is the beginning of our own path and no one else's. Does the child transform and mature? Or is it always the child? In any case, we can make the child robust and balanced by living for oneself and loving self into change. The child senses the camel and lion inside, pays attention to gut feelings regarding a felt sense of being manipulated or controlled as another's pack animal. When the child experiences the anger that accompanies this lack of love or respect – she hears the underground bull or the lion's roar. By recognizing the child's plight, I began to feel a sensation in my gut. I could describe it as a tug. With it, I began to act on my own needs. For me, it was an assimilation of anger, recognizing its gifts of self-definition, my courage to be and to come into my own, separate of my mother, separate from yet within my culture. The child birthed another initiation, personhood as a woman within a patriarchal world where women are still treated as a possession, dismissed, put down, invalidated, non-existent, passed over, silly, shamed, hormonal, sexualized, without opinion, and viewed with distrust, as though she were a witch. We do have magic, though, don't we, girls? As I listened to these deep tones, I entered the mystery of womanhood and the flame of passion grew and grew and became a daughter and garden of bliss.

The Daughter

"A Daughter's Worth"

Daughter, you are the philosopher's delight.
Hidden in your purse is the power of light.
Wear it on your sleeve as tears become
wisdom flowing to your hand.
Do not be sad for you are the
queen of the garden-land.
Your bloom is the smell
of baking bread, the next generation's
repose and yeast.
Daughter, you are not least!
For your faith is our strength
love and hope, O Lady-in-Waiting.
Without you there is no family
gathered round the coals
no carols sung at the years' end
no friends no bonds
no magi to follow what the stars attend.
Yes, the wonder of your body
celebrates shoulders and arms.
Your charms encircle candlelit altars
where prayers arise
flashing eyes following sound
through tears, violence, pain.
Yet Daughter, your bag holds more
than the looking glass of change.

The daughter symbol, innocent and unaware, is like Persephone before Hades abducted and raped her, before she is mourned by Demeter, causing the whole world to wither. Harding says that in women's mysteries, the maiden may have to free herself from Hades under her own efforts.

In Greek mythology, she is called the Kore who returns to the upper world to her mother, Demeter, the Great Mother, year after year. The Kore's task is to die to her immature self to be reborn as a mature woman. This inner drama, shown in dreams, meets the outer as the woman must learn to love her man not just for sexuality or what he can do for her but for who he is as a real, fallible person.[142] As Kore, perhaps Persephone drops into other realities, dark and deep where she sheds scorn, even hatred of womanly qualities woven imperceptibly in convention. In my generation many women, including myself, attempted to identify with manhood rejecting the feminine. Nails, shopping, creating, gardening, rest, clearly were out. Only work, success, and how we looked on the outside mattered. But maturity, maturity as a female, the one including Demeter, was a holding of new, inner values, a sweetness toward my womanhood, toward the daughter within me.

Although my outer world was still a mess as far as my marriage and career during this time, my inner world changed. I embraced the grandmother, child, and daughter. An inner family or cast of characters petitioned me to change my attitude toward myself. They inducted volition. As a result, my feelings and how I was treated by my spouse mattered. This is not to say he was totally at fault. My own baggage prevented a connection with him even with marital therapy. The attack of the World Trade Center also marked the destruction of my marriage on 9/11/2001. I decided life was too short to stay miserable. We divorced. I grieved my mistakenness and I continued to let the images speak in a twilight language, one not easily deciphered, so I could move forward.

CHAPTER 8: FRUITION

Goddess archetypes in dreams urge the female to flower, then bear fruit. Of all goddess archetypes, Mary is the most familiar in the West. Maybe that's why a person called Mary visited so often in dreams. But I can only wonder. In one dream, she was with full and empty cake domes. The full one had rosemary bread in it. She offered it to me in a different form. As I explored the empty dome, the theme of emptiness and emptying, and purification arose. Perhaps the process of purification is stripping away all I am not. On the other hand, it may be understanding who and what I am. Thankfully goddesses of equality also arrived so I could feel some shred of authenticity. It seems they wanted me to know the truth. I had a breakthrough while I was writing, however, that sent me to a Jungian therapist. I discovered a secret I suspected that was hidden in my personal unconscious. It is my hope you too can heal by learning the mysterious twilight language of dreams.

The unconscious contains opposites, striving for reconciliation – Creator and creature, love and hate, female and male, birth and death, optimism and pessimism, trust, and betrayal. When these seeds as opposites are harmonized, we begin to grow. But these seeds are packed tightly, each struggling for light and root, each wanting to be a continuation of a process begun long ago. The most deeply buried seed, however, is the rose, sleeping in environments without warmth, light, or water, entirely covered by weeds.

Sometimes the overgrowth is so thick we cannot find the garden let alone the blossom. The garden walls, once a lacy pattern of white marble, hide beneath thorns and thicket. The fountain is dry and without fish. No longer does its gleeful flow open us to its expression of victory.

Rose seeds can nonetheless be replanted without the original roots. If the rose goes to seed, it can be taken from the blossom's hips, the fruit of the rose. Oh, the seed will have to wait a cold season before it can sprout. It will need much care because the seed is susceptible to damping-off and powdery mildew diseases. But once a new root forms, if you are careful, you can transfer it to sterile soil and ready it for flowering. Just don't expect the same color, pattern, or shape of the plant's parent. Remember, the seed can grow without the old roots. Once it sprouts, and over a period of three to five years, you may find a rose that is special.[143] Within you is the seed of this rose. By listening to the images, the rose, born through the hips, bears fruit.

Goddess archetypes

As noted earlier, I noticed two personages, Rose and Mary. Mary generally had golden hair, and was a maiden, daughter, guide, or friend. "The Friend," according to Estés, is one of the many names of the Wild Woman archetype who emerges from the psychoid unconscious, the deepest, instinctual level of soul.[144] She could also be representative of the Greek goddesses, such as Artemis, or Aphrodite, but I had an affinity for the Christian Mary when I dreamt of her, although she was as distant as close.

In *The Myth of the Goddess*, for example, the authors say Mary was created by men of the church. Her image made earthy women impure and their bodies and sexuality sinful. Similarly, this constructed image robbed women of their rightful power. While Mary is free from any stain, according to the model of perfection made by men of the New Testament, she nonetheless may be regarded as a new form of the Great Mother, Eve, and a resurgence of the goddess. For example, in the last 1,000 years, 21,000 visions of Mary were logged. Between 1928 and 1971, there were 210. Mary as goddess is likened to water, the womb, and called "Stella Maris," or star of the sea. She is traced backward to Aphrodite, also born of sea foam, and to the ever-changing yet stable phases of the moon and the tides. In other words, Mary, arising from the depths of the waters, is none other than the Great Goddess.[145]

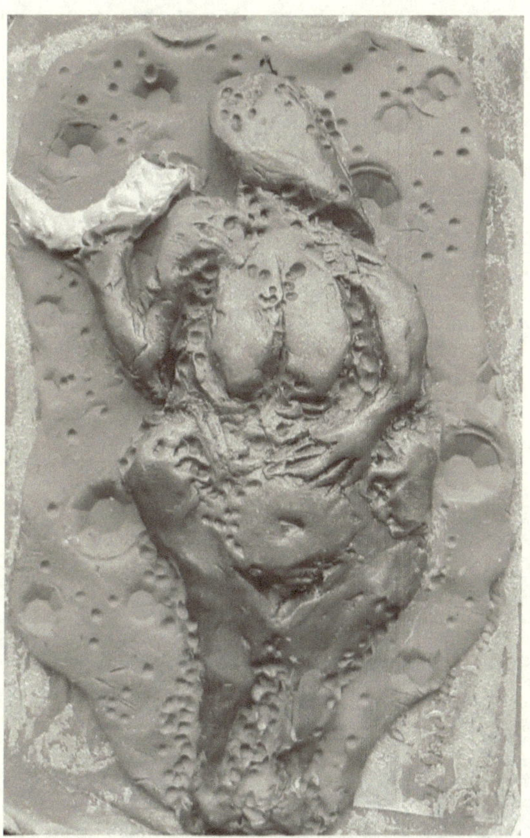

Figure 41. "Artist Trading Card" (2007), after the Goddess of Laussel, 22,000–18,000 BC BC

Figure 42. "Mary of the Watery Moon Float"

Figure 43. "Mary of Lourdes Float"

Figure 41 was created after a rock-carving picture probably from Joseph Campbell's book, *Primitive Mythology.* Like the moon the goddess is holding, I noticed Mary standing on one during a visit to Ajijic, in Jalisco, Mexico. I wondered what it meant. Could Mary still be telling us through art, that the goddess, related to the moon, here the dark moon, and brown skin, is still present? She appeared with light skin and on a white moon as well on street corners. Before the Day of the Dead descendants of the Coco Indians follow floats, one titled, "Mary of Lourdes." They celebrated her, dancing, drumming, and in feathered headdress. The locals, who are now Catholic, may know the goddess but embrace her as Mary.

Figure 44. "Indigenous Dancers," Ajijic, Mexico

Rose, on the other hand, was older and usually had red hair. By contemplating Mary and Rose, I came to understand the two sometimes melt into one whom I call Rosemary. According to Rosicrucian thinking, there exists a connection to Rose and Mary, in the names attributed to her such as the medieval title, *Rosa Mariea* and *Marien Roselan* the German title of Mary, the virgin.[146] She spoke to me in the following dream: I was in a Victorian (olden) type home. There was a round, flat loaf (old world) of bread under a cake dome. I sampled it. Then I'm looking at another that is empty. An older woman, around sixty-five, said, "It's all gone. It was rosemary pumpernickel. They made me a shirt from it, see?" She wore a black floral lace blouse. "Try some," she said, and ripped off some from her sleeve. I added butter, tasted it, and thanked her (Figure 45).

This dream may indicate I am leaving a mother and daughter stage behind, becoming the carline. Demetra George adds other mysteries to this image. As Hekate Triformis, often displayed in art with three heads, Hekate rules heaven, earth, and the underworld. Her nature includes Selene, goddess of the full moon; Artemis of the crescent moon; and Hekate, the waning moon. As the Triple Moon Goddess, Hekate mirrored phases of a woman's life, Persephone, as daughter, Demeter, as mother, Hekate, as crone and grandmother.[147] The rosemary plant behind her is green and suggests a garden, repeated by the dark, floral shirt. Rosemary as a flower is an alexipharmic;[148] that is, an antidote to poison, according to Jung. Women suffer many poisons, but the goddesses offer us relief. Through her we may find a relation with the Creator, to nature, to our bodies. Unlike the Old Testament's edicts that God is beyond and demands following the law perfectly, she seems to be saying healing includes this triple nature. By embracing Hekate's influence, I therefore can accept aging and depend upon Rosemary's guidance.

Figure 45. "Rosemary"

Returning to the image, Rosemary is illuminated with a crown of nine. The halo looks like ears of corn emanating from her head. Is she the corn mother? Ceres, Demeter, and Isis are grain goddesses. Moreover, Rabbi Dr. Hillel ben David says nine is associated with the Hebrew letter, Tet. This is called gematria, an interchange of Hebrew letters and numbers whose relationships deepen symbolic meaning. Letters are also designated to the energy centers or emanations of God on the Tree of Life called the Sephirah. Tet, as such, is related to Yesod, the ninth Sephirah on the Tree of Life. Yesod means "foundation" and is above the tenth Sephirah, Malchut, or Earth. One of the other meanings of Tet is a "hidden, inverted beneficence."[149] As a divine intercessor, Rosemary, therefore, seems to poise herself closely to earthly creatures. Rosemary also might be associated with the whirlwind image shown earlier.

Rose, on the other hand, is related to symbolism of the Hebrew letter, Yod. *The Zohar*, a book studied by Kabbalists, talks about Yod being black and lovesick for her Beloved (like the Shulamite of the Gnostics). Yod is like a comma but elevated. It is a point. This "point is the 'inner point,' which is the same as the 'inner rose,' the 'community of Israel,' the 'Bride.' Further attributes of the rose are sister, companion, dove, perfect one, twin."[150] She sounds like Sophia, goddess of wisdom. Has she always been with me, waiting to flower in my heart?

Kabbalistic emptiness

The Rosemary dream also contained other symbols, some repeated, some new. The domes were new but expressed the opposites, empty and full. According to author Daniel C. Matt, concepts of emptiness or nothingness, similarly, are mentioned in Jewish mysticism. For example, the crown or top Sephirah is called Keter, Ayin, or Nothingness. Further, "The word *kabbalah*, means 'receiving ...'"[151] He states mystics believed there is a timeless dimension dynamically moving into the now if we are open to it. More importantly, kabbalists believe the male form of God has a feminine counterpart, the Shekinah. This word, Shekinah, means "divine immanence" and is the tenth sephirah, earth or Malchut. Like Jung, Kabbalists believe we can have a direct encounter with God who desires human beings to participate in the fruition or fulfillment of the divine here on Earth. In other words, God requires us for completion.[152] The word Ayin, furthermore, is called a Nothingness, a simplicity of wisdom and becoming that cannot be known and destroys thought.[153] Perhaps the

Shekinah receives Nothingness, the presence of God, on Earth (Malchut) from Tet or Yesod, the Sephirah above.

Gnostic emptiness

Another comparison of the void or emptiness is in *The Red Book*, where Jung's inner figure, Philemon, in the "First Sermon of the Dead" speaks of the Gnostic Pleroma. The Pleroma is described as empty and full. There are no forms in this uncreated, infinite empty because the opposites cancel each other out. There is no good or bad, living or dead, light or dark, hot or cold, or any opposite in this region.[154] The Pleroma has equivalencies to the Tibetan Bardo, a state of preexistence, containing all history, an underlying wholeness, devoid of thinking and being, the beginning and end; yet the Pleroma permeates everyone and everything, Jung wrote in *Answer to Job*.[155] Consequently a similarity can be noted between the annihilation of thought in Kabbalistic Nothingness and the canceling out of the opposites in the Gnostic Pleroma.

Buddhist emptiness

The doctrine of emptiness additionally is part of Buddhism. We are said to be empty of self. There is no *one* self, instead just a mind, body, and label. Though it appears so, we are not static. The "I" that receives the body, mind, and label is dependent on causes and conditions and is dynamically part of dependent arising. Dependent arising is about causes and conditions breaking into the life stream from past actions called karma. The aim of Buddhist practice is to purify the "I" of ignorance (the thought that I am separate, operate under my own power, and that I own my body, mind, and objects) and enter the emptiness where Buddha became enlightened. My teacher, Gelek Rimpoche, described emptiness as full.

Emptiness is addressed in the Heart Sutra, a teaching and prayer Buddha gave his disciple, Avalokitesvara. It begins with the statement, "Form is not different from emptiness. Emptiness not different from form. Form is the emptiness. Emptiness is the form ... not born, not annihilated, not tainted, not pure ... no suffering, no cause of suffering, no nirvana, no path; no wisdom, also no attainment because no non-attainment ..." Here again we have the cancelling of the opposites and the destruction of thought as mentioned above. On the other hand, the Heart Sutra is the perfection of transcendent wisdom and it refers to the Sanskrit word, Prajnaparamita, who is the Great Mother and mother of the buddhas. She comes in many forms.

Closely related to Prajnaparamita is a female deity, called a *dakini*. Although there are differing dakinis, depending on the Buddha family or their level of enlightenment, she is displayed as red in my own practice, called Vajrayogini. In *Women who Run with the Wolves*, Estés additionally mentions the dakini as a Wild Woman archetype, who installs knowing to the woman, so she learns to howl loudly when the moon is just right.[156] In my own Vajrayogini (dakini) practice, she is a fierce, triumphant maiden of sixteen. Her age suggests she is like the Kore, the daughter. On her left shoulder is a staff, called a katanga, representing the male energy. In *Women of Wisdom*, Tsultrim Allione writes that the katanga symbolizes a woman's wholeness, independent from a man, and not needing to take masculine energy from him because she has it herself. She adds that in the West, we have no symbols like the dakini, so we can invoke our power. "Women are not given encouragement to see themselves positively when they are assertive and angry. They are taught to be docile and never to threaten."[157]

Figure 46. "Vajrayogini"[158]

Buddhism is practiced differently throughout the world because Buddha taught to the spiritual capability of the student. Therefore, the small vehicle, the great vehicle, and the diamond vehicle spread over the globe. For example, in Thailand and Cambodia, the small vehicle is practiced, the path of the solitary realizer. Likewise, many people in the United States practice this type of Buddhism using mindfulness. In Japan, however, people sit for long periods of time in Zen temples and use koans – mind-confounding statements like "what is the sound of one hand clapping?" – as practice. It is a form of the great vehicle. In Tibet, Buddhism from India evolved from the path of the small vehicle into mahayana (great vehicle) and vajrayana (diamond vehicle) practice. Mahayana Buddhism is about increasing love and compassion.

Bodhisattvas progress on their paths to enlightenment and vow to reincarnate on Earth until everyone is enlightened. This can take myriad lifetimes. Vajrayana, however, is called the "quick path," meaning enlightenment might happen in only one lifetime or in at least sixteen. Working with the dakini, however, requires initiation into tantric path.

After studying the first two forms of Buddhism and meditating for some time, the guru allows the tantric initiation to take place in the Yellow Hat or Gelug tradition of the Dalai Lama. Here the practitioner needs a teaching, an oral transmission in Tibetan, and an initiation from a qualified teacher (in my case, Gelek Rimpoche, my guru). By doing a retreat after the initiation, the practitioner can more intensely connect with the dakini. After about six weeks, I completed my retreat in my meditation room while working full time. I ate, worked, prayed, visualized, and said mantras, 100,000 of them for Vajrayogini. About another 25,000 other mantras were required for the retreat, and these were counted on a mala. While saying mantras, I learned I could also read and practice reasonings on emptiness. I mainly used one called the sevenfold reasoning.

Although it is discussed in the *Supplement to (Nāgārjuna's) "Treatise on the Middle Way"* by Chandrakirti, Jeffrey Hopkins, author and interpreter for the Dalai Lama, further investigates the reasoning with the image of a chariot. Hopkins offers clues to how to meditate after citing other Buddhist authors and using his own examples. Although I pondered his book, *Emptiness Yoga*, long before the retreat, understanding escaped me. I wasn't alone. There were many glazed-over eyes in discussion groups after emptiness teachings were given by my guru. The reasoning is as follows:

> The chariot is not asserted to be other than its parts,
> Nor non-other. It also does not possess them.

It is not in the parts, nor are the parts in it.
It is not the mere collection [of its parts],
Nor is it [their] shape.
[The self and the aggregates are] similar.[159]

When I sat there going over it many times using Hopkins's examples and visualizing myself in a pile of not-me, I disappeared. Similarly, the walls and floor disintegrated. It felt a little like I was riding the Rotor at Euclid Beach where the centrifugal force held me against the wall while the floor dropped down. I couldn't be certain that anything had solidity, much less that I had an ego. Of course, it didn't last and focusing my attention didn't seem to improve much afterward, but it gave me a glimpse, perhaps, of how to empty myself, expelling some ignorance.

Kenosis as emptying

Another way to think about emptying, or stripping away all we are not, is called kenosis. Going to the bathroom, cleaning, and going on a diet (making the belly empty) are repeated, related dream themes in my journals that may symbolize emptying. Likewise, in Kabbalah, one of the top Sephiroth on the Tree of Life, Da'at, is called the empty room. I've long wondered what this means. There is a term called "kenosis" that I learned from Thomas Merton in *The Silent Life.* It means the emptying of our own will to allow God's will to enter. Emptying might have other meanings, however. It may indicate that purification is needed or occurring, the ego is like excrement, or we are getting into our "shit." That is our dissociated feelings, parts, and memories. Perhaps it is letting go of control and trusting in life as well as inner guidance. Following the angel's voice creates the space of unknowing. Space is an image for Nothingness, emptiness, or Pleroma. It is as if creativity and dream work open us to this "place."

Emptying shadow and persona

Similarly emptying may suggest the vacating of unconscious contents in dreams as Jung's concept of shadow, a complex. The shadow, according to Jungian author Daryl Sharp, includes opposites of good and bad either repressed or not recognized. The shadow can act like "the whole of the unconscious" that we project on others,[160] parts of ourselves we began to deny as children, the unsanctioned, shameful parts we don't like as was discussed in previous chapters but it can be positive traits as well.

The shadow or personal unconscious may also contain conditioning. Conditioning is the assimilation of cultural unconscious attitudes and beliefs taught from parents. We have political leanings and judgments about feelings because of conditioning. For example, women are taught anger is bad, so we learn to smile when angry and don't feel. Anger is in a dissociated state, in other words, discharged into the body, where the woman is unaware when she is angry. Or she is angry much of the time because she won't say she is out loud. Furthermore, when we exclude anger, it becomes a volcano that unexpectedly blows up often with someone other than the source of the resentment. Shadow, therefore, likely contains unwanted feelings.

At other times weak parts, like the child, are banned and designated to shadow. Child parts want to be heard, held, loved. Often, they are scared. In dialog with dreams, we can lift this weakness to the light and develop kindness toward these parts. On the other hand, one such part may be labeled as "childish" when what is needed is vulnerability. I happened to be a parent to my mother and had to look after siblings. I didn't get to be a child, nor to be playful. After all parents, at lease mine, were not.

With shadow are behaviors we don't like, like being controlling. I projected this on my boss, for example, and didn't like her. Controlling gets shoved into the dark, but with awareness we may find our dislike of this person is the same as our dislike of a parent and is part of us. If we use our inner ears to hear the shadow, we can dispel behaviors that don't contribute to our personhood.

While weak parts may be in shadow, the persona, or mask, contains what I am now about to describe in more detail. Sharp describes persona as the "I," usually ideal aspects of ourselves, that we present to the outside world," like a mask used in a play to indicate a role, a "protective covering" helpful in social situations.[161] But if we can differentiate the ego from the persona, we no longer act on expectations of the collective and no longer do or think what we "should."[162]

The persona is even more difficult to empty and peel away. This is because we can't see it and we look from it, as if our identity. As I am not a certified Jungian, this is my own take on it. My understanding is that it is like a self we try to maintain, mentioned in Chapter 1, related to self-esteem. Children obtain "high self-esteem" when they get an "A," become a cheerleader, or get a first prize in an art competition, for example. Another way to look at this is self-concept or the opinions and labels we attach to the ego. These thoughts and opinions eventually become stories linked to negative events. I thought, for instance, "Daddy doesn't like me," because he would take my sister on his lap and call her "princess." My pet name, however, was "chunk of chocolate." This event evolved into the "I'm a failure" story. To compensate for this, I decided I must look good, not only to dad but to everyone. It isn't a choice to look good because I feel good about myself; instead it became an obsession beyond style. It was one that drove me with a whip. I had to keep getting smarter to look good. I had to exercise and monitor my weight to look good. I had to become successful to look good, including having a too expensive home and a perfect yard. Yet he just wouldn't give me the recognition I wanted. I begged him, for example, to see me walk for my master's degree, as the first in my family to obtain one. Even though he owned his own business, lived in the area, and wasn't traveling on business, he refused. The excuse was, it was on a Monday night, so he couldn't come. His non-attendance, to me, confirmed his dislike as well as my unworthiness. Consequently, my mask, unseen and unknown, was now cemented in place.

Shakespeare's statement "All the world's a stage" is so true. The comic-tragic symbol of theater is the mask. It represents a performance, not the truth. The mask prevents self-knowledge, and that is the tragedy. Instead, we think high self-esteem must be maintained at any price. Performing becomes addiction and perfectionism. We think we must look good to others to be loved. As a woman, we may become anorexic; as a man, a workaholic; as a gay man, a buff. It becomes a never-ending cycle of seeking love externally but not knowing it internally. It begins with feelings of unworthiness and shame and reaching for what will make us feel better or more in control. The woman with anorexia gets to look down at others who can't control food intake like her. She is a star just as much as Serena Williams. The cost is her death. The workaholic's payoff is he gets to be a "big wig" and amass wealth. The cost is his wife and children when they leave him. Then he works more because he's ashamed and lonely and has a heart attack. The spiritually empty individual strives for outer approval and sadly, exchanges the inner call for addiction.

In graduate school, I saw my perfect persona breakthrough in a "Draw a Person" exercise. Usually the artist will be drawing herself, although she doesn't recognize this. But the art is a revelation. I drew a ballet dancer on point. I wanted to have high self-esteem, but self-esteem is a dirty, judgmental term. There is always someone better or someone worse. Yet in the Western world we wear this face. I remember author Kristin Neff writing about this problem in *Self-Compassion.* She reported the Dalai Lama in one of his Mind and Life conferences asking his interpreter to define low self-esteem. It was a foreign concept to him. A group of American scientists were in the audience. He asked, "How many of you have low self-esteem?" Like me as the ballet dancer, almost all of them raised their hands. Unless this is unearthed, we cannot begin to have self-acceptance, to love this enactment and then to let it go. Self-acceptance is clean – and it is realistic. My guru taught that we cannot have compassion for others until we have it for ourselves. A tight-fitting persona prevents either and here is the divine comedy. The mask is a falsity.

Attachment theory and persona

Persona in my view can similarly be understood in the light of attachment theory. This theory, devised and published as a book by John Bowlby in 1993, proposes three main types of attachment: secure, insecure, and avoidant. In the strange situation experiment, Mary Ainsworth, a follower of Bowlby, observed children in a lab setting from nine to eighteen months interacting with their caregivers in 1970. Here a mom and her child enter a room, and the mom and child play with toys. A stranger enters then mom leaves (strange situation can be viewed on YouTube). There is more to the experiment, but what happens is that if the child is secure, it will cry and search for mom, and when mom comes back, the child allows mom to comfort him. The avoidant child will neither search or cry but continue to play with toys when mom leaves and when she returns. With anxious attachment, however, the child will cry and search and even allow mom to pick her up, but then will arch away from mom and try to get down. This is called protest behavior. Part of the mask is not having an awareness that protest behavior becomes resentment and acting on it further erodes self-esteem. I wonder if the child part inside, insecurely attached, or avoidant, remains angry because the mother never bonded to her.

In insecurely attached individuals, pleasing behaviors may become part of persona. When I studied case histories for my counseling license, for example, most of the depressed women mentioned were people-pleasers, unaware of their mask. The child and later adult want to please to keep attachment figures close. She wants to look nice because she believes she is unlovable underneath. Then she tries harder. When attention is not reciprocated, however, she feels more and more resentment. My anxious attachment similarly contributed to people-pleasing behaviors. Since I didn't trust in relationships, it seemed the only option.

My caretaker mask emerged when I, as a small child, must have been afraid my mother would die of sadness. I needed her to survive, literally, so she could provide food and shelter. I became the perfect helper so she wouldn't be sad. I didn't want others to feel sad or unrecognized, either, so I overdid for siblings, friends, lovers, and co-workers. The persona, self-concept, and driver of self-esteem was ignorance, a performance, and an exhausting one. Then I would get angry (protest behavior) when my efforts weren't returned. Reciprocation wasn't happening. S l o w l y, I loosened the mask by doing less for others. Moreover, out loud I said I didn't like that I was doing most of the contacting and inviting. However little if anything changed with those who had known me at an early age.

This caused me tremendous inner turmoil as I look back. These behaviors eroded my self-respect and kept me in the victim role, without choice. Relationship and truth at odds, subservience lost. The inner voice said, "No More!" I asserted with friends and family members clearly and ungracefully. My passivity erupted at last. Stating the emotional truth out loud to them was like facing a monster or withstanding Hurricane Katrina. My heart pounded, hoping they would grasp what I was saying but instead they became angry. I let them go; they let me go. I felt sad and guilty afterward. The sadness was about loss– the loss of lifelong relationships and the loss of my persona. The culture complex still gripped me with the idea that women are sinful and "should" be nice, not honest, hence guilt. Perhaps Artemis, in her shadow aspect, was insisting on equality rather than relationship. She blessed me with a plethora of dreams, however, once I acted after a long, long draught. I chose the way of not-knowing.

By listening intently to the inner images, the unconscious canalizes into and enlarges our ego. This includes reviewing dreams and comparing symbols that repeat. Both in the Rosemary dream and a dream in 1995, for example, appeared sleeves, black velvet, and a purse. In the 1995 dream, I selected a colorful and black velvet dress with a small purse sewn into a sleeve, to wear for a play, the dress of persona, of performance. Wearing your heart on your sleeve means to be open and honest. Perhaps my essence and worth had to do with emotional honesty, that there is much value, gold, and coin in that. A purse is a container; it hides valuables. Maybe the Philosopher's Stone. As a pouch, it may represent a womb where the ego gains in value, as it lives in service to the Self. Edinger states, "All psychic contents have substance, so to speak, if they are experienced as objectively real. What then distinguishes the psychic substance of consciousness? Consciousness is psychic substance connected to an ego,"[163] a golden substance, indeed.

Goddesses of equality and assertion

As I attended and studied, I observed various myths living in me as if I were an actor in their play. The myths of Lilith and Artemis, for example, affected me by insisting on fairness in relationships. The black velvet, especially the floral one pictured in Rosemary's shirt and the black velvet dress, may be about the Dark Moon Goddess, Lilith, Adam's first wife, who flew away from the Garden of Eden (floral and dark). Demetra George states Lilith resides collectively in our female shadow, as a remnant of the goddess religion after the patriarchy defeated it. Created as an equal to Adam in Genesis 1, the stories say in rebellion of sexual and other forms of domination by Adam, Lilith fled. She was therefore demonized as a witch, a child-killer, and a hag as power shifted from female to male. Yet our inner work can reclaim her in three steps, George writes. First, we need to examine our domination by others. This is about no longer suppressing unacceptable, rebellious parts, or by being nice. In this phase resentment may explode because of suppressed energy in our shadow as we see and speak the truth. We no longer pretend in relationships whether an intimate partner, boss, teacher, or group.

In the second stage, feelings of devastation and rejection abound, as we stand up for the self, are belittled and betrayed, and then feel shame afterward. Revenge in many cases rises from our shadow parts. By maintaining integrity to the self, we lose connection to others and feel lonely. Yet while in the desert exile, the Lilith within restores her inner strength to overcome the need for other's approval.

The final stage is about Lilith using her curved knife to peel off what disguises her true self, her bondage ends, and she is redeemed. By speaking our truth, we are still unrelated to society, but we can be transformed by the Tibetan Black

Dakini who cuts away everything that does not serve our individuality. Here we are secure in speaking up for the true self and do not pretend to gain acceptance. From this position we are no longer vulnerable to those who might manipulate or diminish us. Eventually we develop methods to solve conflict instead of fleeing from it without belittling others and come to consensus, the experience of one-ness, no-self. This is the pattern of Lilith, the Dark Moon Mother.[164]

Jean Shinoda Bolen in *Goddesses in Older Women*, similarly, reveals that Artemis as an archetypal pattern, also insists on fairness, independence, and sisterhood, as her attendants were young girls she protected. She was also athletic, goal-oriented, and spiritually connected to nature and wildlife, either hiking or horseback riding. She, like a working mother, feels as though everyone wants to suckle her many breasts, limiting her freedom. But as she enters the crone phase, the Artemis within can think young and may wish to serve others by coaching younger women. She may also further the women's movement or engage in the climate crisis. Her shadow side, however, was about punishment, intolerance, being quick to anger and subsequent remorse. However, because she had the capability to reflect as a Waning Moon Goddess, she could learn humility and patience, taking the advice of Hekate before taking a course of action that impacts others or self negatively.[165]

When we become aware of inner forces, we no longer pretend or need to wear a mask for approval. We can voice our truth after thinking about consequences and become more compassionate. My people-pleasing mask prevented me from speaking up gracefully. However, when I asserted early in the relationship, I was successful. When I found a loving partner, who respected me and served as a secure base (now of seventeen years), I learned to trust, overcoming the anxious attachment pattern. "Having a partner who is inconsistently available or supportive can be a truly demoralizing experience that can literally stunt our growth and stymie our health," say Amir Levine and Rachel S. F. Heller,[166] authors *of Attached: The New Science of Adult Attachment and How It Can Help You Find - and Keep - Love.* Because of my inner companions, I am free to be authentic and to spend time with family and friends who do reciprocate and are secure bases, allowing me to flourish. Therefore, protest behavior on my part was immature, perhaps as the daughter, but the mature woman as Rose knows I have the right to security and assertion at the same time without forgetting restraint.

In another layer different from the mask, probably from the personal unconscious, memories hidden from me since childhood arose while writing this material. Perhaps these were the "Precious Memories" Andy Griffith mentioned in Chapter 6. Only when the woman feels safe can images of amnesia float into consciousness as an emptying. This safety and sense of equality in intimate relationship, friends, job, and family allowed this, I believe, for me.

Emptying of sexual trauma

As the shamanka, I stalked my journal dream themes in 2019 while writing this material. The energy in dream feels chaotic, I note several times, with instances of betrayal, divorce, invasion into my dream apartment, stuck legs, leg messages, leggings, trees whose metal guards were cutting into the bark, children I was babysitting, children wanting me to hold them, and three boys (I played with three boys as a child, one who I will call Ricky). One dream was more specific. It was about a childhood friend crying about children being mistreated. My friend said her therapist couldn't treat her anymore because she had blocked the origin of the depression. As I woke, I recalled her sexual abuse.

My angel in active imagination said Ricky raped me; I record it twice within a few months. The first time I recorded the dialogue, it didn't register. Denial is very sneaky. The second time after the dream of children being mistreated, the angel asked me to remember what Ricky did and to give myself time to mourn. This was how I could remove the blockage and move forward. After I followed her advice, my childhood friend who also played with the boys, out of the blue, called me the next day. Quite a synchronicity. I asked her if she thought it could be true Ricky raped me. She replied, "Probably. He did the same to me."

Sadness, loneliness, and anger around this act affected every aspect of my life. I suspected this all along but had no proof or memory of it except playing doctor and Ricky's mother finding us. This is what children do, I thought. While I had five different therapists, either I didn't stay in therapy long enough or since I had amnesia, the abuse remained hidden. A profound, inexplicable pain lingered from the original abuse and the ongoing re-traumatization from the men my broken picker chose. Women unconsciously try to master trauma through reenactment. Yes, all the world is a play, an unconscious one. On the other hand, perhaps I projected my shadow on men. Yet in one way or another the men in my life were emotionally abusive, confirming the belief I was unworthy. This is self-fulfilling prophecy, how belief became expectation. The pain of this unknowing was unendurable and repeated. It was as if I had to create to find some meaning or purpose to my suffering. This was why I recorded my dreams, wrote poetry, and created art. I didn't want anyone to suffer like I had so maybe through creativity and my work as a therapist, I could let other women know they weren't alone, and they weren't powerless.

As a therapist, I learned safety is the first goal in the treatment of trauma. The second and third goals of trauma treatment include mourning and reconnection/ reintegration. Most of the trauma literature notes that fragmentation of the self occurs, scattered into the body and into the unconscious. Colors, smells, movements, time, touch, sound, tastes, and images linked to the event have few if any associative neural networks. The body records the event when the mind and emotions obliterate it. The sufferer has little agency, is in freeze mode and shut down. Alexithymia and fibromyalgia often accompany trauma. The Creator heals, however, in small doses over a long time. I'm sixty-seven and am just now moving to the mourning stage. Emotions aren't connected to the traumatic images yet, but since I've practiced them symbolically, I'm guessing some of the energy secluding the memories lessened.

Because of the angel, I decided to review the images in this book and found they contained the symbolic vocabulary of rape. Dee Spring, author of *Image and Mirage,* studied women's art during treatment at a rape crisis center she directed. She noticed recurring symbols whether the woman was raped as a child or an adult. They are the following:

- a single, red flower (was the grandmother, Rose about this?)
- open mouths in a scream (see Figures 2 and 23)
- fragmentation (see Figure 19)
- the colors of red, black, blue, yellow (see Figures 14, 23, 24, and 25)
- layering (see Figures 18, 19, and 23)
- balloons and floating objects (see Figure 29 and the poem, "Vessel.")

- varying forms of vortex or spirals (see Figures 35 and 31)
- disembodied eyes (see Figure 36)
- circles, and mandalas (see Figures 31 and 33)[167]

Other researchers published graphic indicators of sexual abuse in the latter two bullets. Consequently, Rosemary disclosed a truth hidden for a lifetime.

Twilight language of dreams

Dreams are largely dismissed in our culture because they are hard for the rational mind to understand. Yet dreams, even in the Bible, held importance and give clues. For example, Joseph with the coat of many colors interpreted dreams of his destiny and for the Pharaoh of Egypt, beginning in Genesis 37:3. Joseph heard the twilight voice of images. The dialect doesn't follow chronological order, nor is it clear or bright, like solar, scientific consciousness. It is the crossroad of day becoming night and the border where mind meets dream objects. These representations are a way to hear the divine voice. Twilight thinking notes similarities, not absolute details, like the variants present in myth. For example, in one myth Aphrodite is born of sea foam and in another, born from the embrace of Zeus and Dione. We ponder, we reflect what the images may symbolize, but we never know for sure.

Let me use an example of the twilight language present in dreams. In the first chapter, I discuss the dream image of the crater and the comforter. I painted it and it helped me recall the dream. Then I investigated it. Now let's look at Joseph's coat of many colors. It is like the quilt settling into my "crater dream." Also, in the story of Joseph is a pit, like the crater, where his evil, jealous brothers place him because he has big dreams and is the favorite of their father, Israel. Joseph's brothers sell him into slavery, but he becomes a vizier in

Pharaoh's court, due to his dream interpretations. A silver cup additionally is part of the story of Joseph's reunification with his family.

The Holy Grail is often described as a silver cup, the cup Jesus drank from in the Last Supper. In Chapter 4, Eve holds such a silver cup. These "objects," the pit and krater, the cup and the many-colored coat and quilt, are metaphors for archetypal patterns. The many-colored coat or quilt may represent the Holy Spirit connecting the divine to the creature. The crater and pit seem to be the wounding of the creature by the solar, masculine power necessary for further consciousness; the silver cup, probably a lunar, feminine element, may represent the ego-sacrifice and service to the Self. The silver cup includes a relational, emotionally felt experience. Perhaps this is the knowing-with or being in relation to the Self, according to Edinger. Again, this is a pondering, not a fact or concept, as twilight language is dusky.

The new myth from Jung's work refers to the ego as the vessel for developing consciousness and becoming a bearer of consciousness, so the Holy Spirit is born in the individual.[168] Is the ego the silver cup? Another such question is, what twilight message did Rosemary offer? She resembled a female minister I knew. More than a grandmother, she contained a maiden, giving birth to the new. The dream reminded me of a poem I had written about seven years prior, called "The Daughter's Worth." In writing about the psychological aspects of the Kore, Jung echoes this knowing and rebirth by saying that in every woman resides a mother, but especially later in life, lives a daughter. "The conscious experience of these ties produces the feeling that her life is spread out over generations–the first step towards the immediate experience and conviction of being outside time, which brings with it a feeling of immortality."[169] Rosemary allows a healing where "obstacles are cleared out of the way of the life-stream that is to flow through her," and where she is no longer alone but made whole.[170] This is the fruit, one I offer to you. Let you who have ears, hear!

CHAPTER 9: CREATIVE TOOLS FOR HEALING

Many expressive tools were sprinkled throughout this book. They are offered as methods to access the image nation. Some others follow for the reader to use personally if he or she is without prior art or religious orientation. Dream and visual journals, the use of meditation, art therapy techniques, poetry, and mandalas are some examples. Most importantly, investigate your own image nation.

In the West, where words and the rational approach predominates, our culture is cut off from emotions and soul. This is the bold, masculine way of the patriarchy. It has its place, but it can be dry and spiritually empty. On the other hand, images water the soul. Images offer the silver cup of mana. Mana is defined as "the power of the elemental forces of nature embodied in an object or person."[171] In my opinion, it resides in the painted, drawn, or dream representation as well as within us. It connects us, and we participate with the image nation when using creativity.

Along these same lines, author Owen Barfield, who was a friend of C. S. Lewis, in *Saving the Appearances: A Study of Idolatry*, says, "Original participation is ... the sense that there stands behind the phenomena, *and on the other side of them from man*, a represented, which is of the same nature as man. It was against this that Israel's face was set. The devotee in the presence of the totem feels himself and the totem to be filled with the same 'mana.' They are, 'stopping-laces for mana.'"[172]

In other words, what is on the other side of the represented is like the God-image. The represented could be a tree viewed outside the window or a painting of the tree. Idolatry, on the other hand, is when we take a literal approach to images. A tree is separate from the viewer. It becomes words, leaves, bark, branches, trunk, and roots. Original participation, however, is like pantheism and shamanism. It connects the Creator to the creature through nature. All objects, even the stone, are alive. Nature is meaningful and one with the human. Similarly, in the Bible, humans were created in the image of God. This image within can be heard and felt when we attend or participate with dreams or create. The imagination is like a mirror to the God-image.

In *A Barfield Reader*, editor G. B. Tennyson clarifies the Imagination. He states, "[It is] the chief mode by which the human mind apprehends reality and through which it expands knowledge and awareness. 'The Imagination is a form ... of perception, if you like, a way of apprehending reality which cannot be reformulated in terms of logical sequences. It's not a rule of logic and reason, but it's not unreal for that reason.' The rational faculty can increase understanding, but it cannot increase knowledge; only the Imagination can increase knowledge and expand consciousness."[173]

Remembering dreams is primary in contacting the imagination in my view. When interest is developed toward the unconscious, the image nation sends dreams. They begin to flower as an awareness of another dimension. When in emotional crises, dreams move from flowering to a fruited orchard, helping one know he or she is not alone. Therefore, recording them in a journal is like a modern-day ritual for the practicing shamanka or shaman.

Figure 47: "Dream Giraffe Totem: Stand tall in your inquisitive instinct."

Dream journals

The first way to work with dreams is to say before falling asleep, "I will remember my dreams." Upon waking, don't move and try to remember the dream. Muscle movement erases the memory. Also, keep a pen, flashlight, and notebook within easy reach to write it down as soon as you remember it. Try to note the mood or feeling you have upon waking even if you don't remember the dream. Dreams have far more to do with emotional truth than they do with anything else. Another method I've used to recall dreams is to write a paragraph on any subject before going to sleep. Upon waking write a few words down without thinking and let those associations flow into a paragraph to stimulate recall.

When I first started to record dreams, they were innumerable because they had so long been neglected. At first, dreams will be chaotic, dark, and at times, nightmarish. The unconscious uses this method to get our attention. The dark images, too, may be expressions around superego or parental injunctions that have taught you not to feel, it is dangerous to feel. Like Eve, dark dreams also introduce the descent into the unconscious. Many women's mysteries included the underworld. They will need much sorting. What to keep, what to discard is a little like Psyche's tasks given by Aphrodite, which were to sort a pile of seeds into individual types by sundown. Psyche also had to fill a flask with water in the River Styx (the river in the underworld or land of the dead). Eventually, Psyche completed her tasks, developed daring, and then joined Eros (her lover) on Olympus. Often dreams express mounds of grief. Bear with them. You may want a therapist's help along the way if feelings are too intense. Or you may want to draw a mandala, described later in this section, to contain the feelings for you. When you stick with the image, you, like Psyche, face your fears. You will be guided to manage strong feelings, practicing them first through the image, then again through reflections by writing until you are moved to change your outlook and behavior.

Dreams introduce the image nation, the soul or hidden world, where the female and male share divinity. If we think of the word, hermaphrodite, meaning bisexual, both male and female, the male aspect is Herm or Hermes, the feminine aspect is Aphrodite (Venus in Roman mythology). She, in Greek myth, is the goddess of love, worshipped through the ages as the planet, Venus, both morning and evening star, virgin and whore, kore and mother. Hermes, on the other hand, is the hermaphrodite. As a messenger god, he holds the caduceus, a staff with two entwined snakes, male and female, with wings on top. Like Hermes, the dream image is the messenger, and the healing, like the sign of the physician, at least in the United States.

Hermes, as self-knowledge, is known as lord of the crossroads and god of merchants and thieves. Hiding, he plays with us as a trickster and does magic, the transformation of the female to include the male or vice versa.

The inner feminine plays as well. She conceals herself in dream mysteries and words. MA, for example, presents herself in MAtter, MAterial, imMAge, MAntic (related to divination or prophecy), MAgician, MAge, iMAgination, MAmmary, MAna, MAnna, shaMAnka, shaMAn. Here, the Great Mother has voice even though Christianity emphasizes the male. From the land of the dead, the underworld, the void, emptiness, or the 95 percent dark matter and energy physicists say underlies the universe, comes the symbolic language of soul. Let it instruct you.

Sticking to the image is the best way to work with dreams. Robert A. Johnson, a Jungian analyst, states we can start by writing down associations to the image. For example, the word *children*, as an image in the dream. *Associations to children*: noisy, energetic, cry, shout, playful, creative, innocent, temper tantrum, and vulnerable. Don't add to noisy with other words like traffic, explosion, thunder, etc. Keep going back to what the image of children may represent to you.

After noting associations, you can ask your dream characters what they want and why they are here, using active imagination. Let them answer. You may want to use a different color pen to record their voice or use capitals for them while you use cursive. You don't always have to agree to what dream people want. You can negotiate but let them be heard. In some way, take an action directed by your inner companions so long as it is in accord with your own values.[174]

Meditation

Like the Wizard of Oz, the ego wants to rule, to control unwanted events, emotions, the past, the future, and especially other people. "You must listen," it says. As if at its direction, your thoughts and stories become facts. But we aren't in control of much except our own behavior. Meditation is about observing stories, beliefs, and directives of the ego. And when we sit in the meditative posture, noticing thoughts, we detach from them. The purpose of practice is to witness stories in daily life. We get better and better at this with daily practice. Similarly, the meditator becomes kinder to self and to others. You can find many meditation apps such as Calm. Start slowly, just breathing for three minutes a day. Then add more time to your practice until you reach twenty minutes.

Meditation concentrates the mind; contemplation is similar. For example, Thomas Merton, a Catholic Trappist monk, was described as a contemplative. As a Christian tradition, centering prayer is included in contemplative practice. Here, the practitioner uses an image of a saint and waits for a message. The energy of the otherworldly being speaks in the silence of contemplation. Another way to think about this is with the word *invocation.* In Buddhism we invoke deities or our guru with images. As contemplators, we open ourselves. It takes a long time to allow the energy from these angels to be heard. Allione states this hearing may be attuned to the symbolic dakini language. It is a hidden, visual language, a treasure heard in the twilight.[175]

Drawing is a type of meditation. As such, it is also a kind of focusing in the present moment, where the artist is free of commerce with time. The artist connects to the energy of the model's body or of the objects drawn, painted, or sculpted. Without ego control, life directly flows through. Color additionally concentrates the mind upon emotion, to accept and release sensations from the body. With any form of art or craft, time stands still. Meditators and artists are open, fully, to the present. Sometimes, periods of thoughtlessness occur. This isn't the intention of meditation, however, but it happens.

Poetry

"Companion"
My brother, my friend
who comes again and again
hair curling golden rings
over eyes reticent to the day
yet boundless in their leaping.
It is only with your look
that I glimpse the road's end
only with your touch
the path is cleared of snow
so this weary traveler
can be taken in
warmed by friends
faithful to the fire.
Yes, only your hand uplifts
this heavy vehicle
like a fish reeled from
the river's swollen-fingered grasp
else I drown deep in the vale.
Drawn by your gentle eye
I am clothed in astonishment.

Poetry is simply the evocation of images using words. It connects ideas through associations. Psalms, hymns, and myths take the form of poetry because this type of literature always says more than mere words. The symbolism in dreams also is like poetry. Most of the symbol remains unknown. There cannot be exactness. My poems consisted of dream fragments, repetitions of images and dream themes. I mixed contents from journals, myths, memories, investigations, and drawings. The re-examination of symbols increases insight like a torch in a cave. Use of occasional rhyming also seems to expand the meanings beyond the initial images. Poetry was a way for me to amplify or better understand my dreams, to express my feelings, and to connect with others. In a poetry group I was advised my writing was too esoteric. I kept writing anyway. Although I didn't use it at the time, there is an area of practice called poetry therapy and a National Association for Poetry Therapy. If you want more information about this, you can look online for books, blogs, and other simple exercises to add to your healing tools.

Visual journals

Another way to hear the angel is to keep a visual journal of dreams. A plain, 8-by-11-inch, unlined spiral notebook can be purchased. You may wish to light a candle and play soft music to mark the sacred space before decorating the sketchbook cover. Various torn or cut papers, magazine images, tissue paper, paint, glitter, or other materials can be sealed with Mod Podge, a clear glue. The dream image always will produce more information than just words. But you do not need to be an artist to fashion dream or other pictures! What is important is the process, not the product. The process is like mana, a connection to the inner world.

In the visual journal, try to draw the recalled image, noting color, shape, and movement as best as can be represented or use magazine images if that is less daunting. Also, try to draw or paint dream characters. There are many "how to" drawing books that might help if you wish to use them. I look at Google Images and then draw one that is like my dream. Even the choice of the image will add another layer of meaning. Markers, colored pencils, oil pastels, or watercolors can be combined and are not expensive. Dialogue with the images as if they were a new acquaintance like the example in Chapter 7. Record the conversations on the page facing the art. Or you can write associations, phrases, memories, and root meanings from a dictionary that arise from the image. In other words, open the sketchbook and on one page create the image and on the other, write about it.

Visual journals can include other art therapy techniques. One way is like scribble drawings created as a child. Art therapist Florence Cane, early in the history of art therapy, directed clients to first use wide, swinging movements while standing. Then she asked them to "draw" in the air using the whole body and record the movements on a sheet of paper. After drawing the scribble for thirty seconds or so in a continuous line, clients stopped. Afterward, the paper was turned in all four orientations to locate an image. Then, using the lines as a starting place, she directed patients to create an image.[176] The picture is developed like a camera lens focusing. Emphasize some lines and color over others. If an image isn't apparent, fill in scribbles with different colors and then try to find one. In this way a waking dream might be stimulated from the unconscious. See Figure 29 for an example.

Note the qualities in the image. Give the image a title. A dictionary may be used to locate meanings of the title and root words. Ask the following questions: What do the colors recall? What movements are suggested? Does the image seem on the top or bottom of the paper? Is it toward the right, perhaps moving into the future? Is it centered? Does the image feel light or heavy? What texture does it take? What overall feeling is the image expressing? Dialogue with the image. Ask: "What do you want? Why are you here? What can I do for you?" Use the opposite page to write the dialogue, associations, and root words.

Another method is to cut shapes out of old cereal boxes. Arrange the shapes and trace them in the visual journal. Turn the picture in all four orientations and create an image. After finishing the image, on the opposite page, write your associations to the image. The image above was created with the cereal box, shape technique.

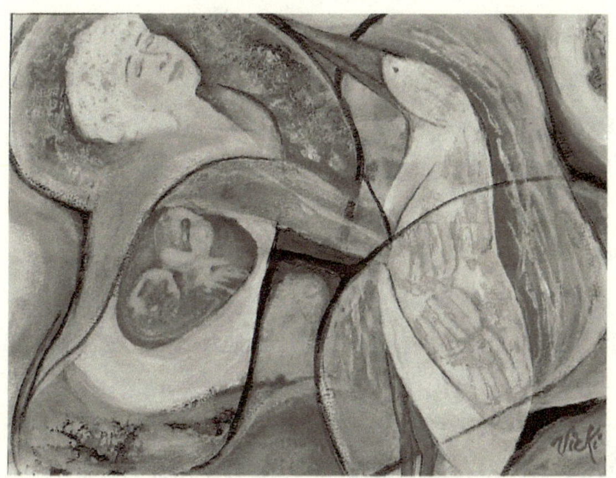

Figure 48. "Creative Heart"

By using a roller filled with paint over materials like corrugated cardboard, found objects, or by drawing into Styrofoam, texture can be created. This is how the orange, for example, was added to the white bird and inside the womb. After I completed the picture, I could see a snake inside. Serpents, the labyrinth of death, the bird, and fish appeared with goddess figures in paleolithic times[177] along with the stork.[178] What is the relation of the snake to the bird, I wondered? Is the serpent about to fly, like Hermes's winged caduceus? Or is the Plumed Serpent, Quetzalcoatl, of the Aztecs here? The bird looks like a stork or an ibis. She is reaching into its heart. Her arm looks fiery. Is the snake rendering the gift of fire? The woman looks as if in ecstasy or a shamanic trance. The ibis is the favorite bird of Hermes.[179] This is how I contemplate images.

You can also draw in your journal using just lines, shapes, and colors with a marker or oil pastel. By rendering differing lines, movements, colors, and shapes, you can give expression to hidden feelings. Write about how the lines and shapes look and what associations they may have for you. See if you can find a feelings list and name the feeling the marks represent. In this way we combine feeling with logic. When we know what the feelings are, we can take care of them by soothing ourselves in a healthy way, by saying, "no," or asking for what we want.

Mandalas

Another way to use art for a beginning artist is to create a mandala. All you need to do is trace a circular form on a page. You can use a plate or anything circular as a template. Try to create some stillness with some deep breathing while listening to soft music. Allow an image to arise. Once you have an image place that in the center. After drawing it, focus on the image for a few moments, then fill in the rest of the circle. If you don't get an image, that's okay, just start in the center with a color you like and begin. Then fill in the circle.

During graduate school, a plethora of mandalas populated my visual journals. The term *mandala,* derived from Sanskrit, means "circle." They can be made with glued tissue and other papers, paints, colored pencils, cray-pas, and glitter glue in any combination. After creating the mandala, give it a title.

Notice what is up, down, to the left or right. Connect the mandala to previous images. In my journal, for example, I say, "I loved playing with the colors. At first it seemed blah, but I just kept adding and softening. It looks like an offshoot of the Hand Flower image I made about a week ago. The petal at the death position is open. The wheel is no longer retrograde as the white lines move it clockwise. The open petal looks like bird wings. Flight in giving up the old. A peacock eye. Seven going to eight. Thought and reaction."

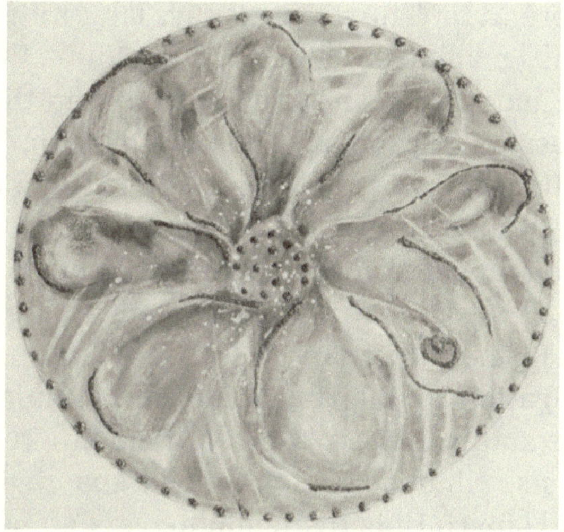

Figure 49. "Wheel Flower"

The mandala ritual initiates a search into the inner world or center. We can observe them in rose windows in churches, as a rosary of repeated prayers, or as a medicine wheel created by the Navajo. It is the visual counterpart of chanting, evoking silence, and quieting the left, verbal hemisphere as all art will, therefore reducing anxiety. Jung was responsible for Western interest in this symbol. He said that they would arise spontaneously in dreams to restore inner balance. Privately he created mandalas and encouraged patients to draw or paint them. The eye as the mandala may open us to divine energy. In Matthew 6:22 (KJV), for example, Jesus said, "The light of the body is the eye: if therefore thine eye be single, thy whole body shall be full of light."

Mandalas serve other purposes, according to Dahlke. He reported that the mandala harmonizes the left hemisphere with the right.[180] Art therapist and author Susanne F. Fincher reports "an undeniable release of tension when making a mandala."[181] Mandalas are tools to re-establish emotional calm.

The Reverend Dr. Laura Artress says labyrinths similarly function as mandalas. Since 2500–2000 BC, people walked the narrow, meandering path to find their center or wholeness. In Europe, the Cretan labyrinth, associated with the Minotaur, was the oldest known type of walked mandala. Yet labyrinths can be found in many traditions, such as the elongated Jewish mystical Kabbalah, or Tree of Life. They were also part of ancient Rome, England, Scandinavia, and Germany.[182] A labyrinth is like a circumnavigation or pilgrimage around Mount Kalish in Tibet, for example. This outer sacred mountain is revered by Buddhists, Hindus, and others in the region, while walking the labyrinth is the feminine version of the inner circular mountain.

Artress came to Ursuline College during the dedication ceremony to the labyrinth and educated us how to utilize it while I was a student. She, for example, asked the audience to sit quietly prior to entry and to formulate a question. Once entering the circle, she instructed us to attend to pace and body movement. Once in the center, she suggested facing in all the cardinal directions and even lying down to receive an answer to the question to simply allow healing energies to penetrate the body. On the way out, I think she said to practice gratitude. This, therefore, was use of the kinetic and bodily sense, rather than the visual sense, as in creating a mandala in a journal.

Joan Kellogg and Susanne F. Fincher are two authors who write about specific forms and colors in mandalas. Perhaps they can hint at possible meanings for yours as you associate what the colors mean personally to you. Fincher says the mandala suggests maturational development of the human species, cultures, and of the individual. Originating as far back as Neolithic man, the mandala symbolized an association with the sun and moon and consciousness and unconsciousness. Use of the mandala may have assisted early man "to develop their thinking beyond purely instinctive levels" and to "step from instinctive group mind to individual consciousness of self."[183]

The artist of life withstands fear and creates without knowing the outcome, is driven by demonic powers to the edge, to the dreaded state of mind. Using the circle, however, hermetically encloses the personality so it is safe to reorganize, to create, to purify and empty outdated modes of existence. In many traditions, circles are supreme symbols of protection, blending being and non-being. As such they are a path of courage, beauty, generosity, and order.

Attend to your dreams and images so you can find out who you really are. Carl Jung calls us to individuate, to become whole, through dream, art, and learning. He wrote for intellectuals who were curious and who felt the Christian myth no longer had meaning. Joseph Campbell, another hunter, also studied Jung. Campbell points out two main mythologies developed in the primitive world, that of planters and that of hunters. The planters, with priests, law, and group norms, suppressed self-discovery, while the hunters, who participate in initiatory solitude, are supported by the group to discover their own divine image and path.[184]

Even now in polar regions, women's magic is powerful and "female shaman are numerous and highly regarded."[185] Hunt the image as a shamanka. Hunters are called to individuate. Planters do not dare. The angel whispers and will wave at twilight.

Will you hear her?

ENDNOTES

Introduction

1 Deborah B. Robinson, *The Sámi of Northern Europe* (Singapore: Times Edition, 2002), 14.

2 Neil Kent, *The Sámi People of the North: Social and Cultural History* (London: Hurst & Company, 2014), 5-82.

3 Wikipedia contributors, "Sámi people," *Wikipedia, The Free Encyclopedia,*

https://en.wikipedia.org/w/index.php?title=S%C3%A1mi_people&oldid=909230155 https://en.m.wikipedia.org (accessed August 8, 2019).

Chapter 1

4 C. G. Jung, *Aion: Researches into the Phenomenology of the Self,* trans., R.F.C. Hull, Bollingen series 9 (Princeton, NJ: Princeton University Press, 1979), 34.

5 Willis Barnstone, *The Restored New Testament: A New Translation with Commentary Including the Gnostic Gospel Thomas, Mary and Judas* (New York: W. W. Norton, 2009), 582.

6 *Merriam-Webster's Collegiate Dictionary,* 10th ed. (Springfield, MA: Merriam-Webster, Inc., 1993), s. v. "crater."

7 M.-L. Von Franz, "The Process of Individuation," *Man and His Symbols,* eds. Carl C. Jung and M.-L. Von Franz (New York: Dell, 1964), 169.

8 Katherine Tingley, "What is Theosophy?" theosophy-nw.org. https://www.theosophy-nw.org (accessed January 6, 2020).

9 I. M. Oderberg, "The Quest: From Simple 'Fool' to Grail Servant," theosophy-nw.org. https://www.theosophy-nw.org/theosnw/world/anceur/eu-imo.htm (accessed January 6, 2020).

10 C. G. Jung, *Psychology and Alchemy*, 2nd ed., trans. R. F. C. Hull, Bollingen series 20 (Princeton, NJ: Princeton University Press, 1953), 299.

11 Johannes van Oort, "The Holy Spirit as feminine: Early Christian testimonies and their Interpretation," Theological Studies, Vol. 72, No. 1, 2016, https://hts.org.za/index.php/hts/article/view/3225/7763 (accessed January 7, 2020).

12 M. Esther Harding, *The I and the Not-I: A Study in the Development of Consciousness* (Princeton, NJ: Princeton University Press, 1965), 136.

13 Thomas L. Moore and Douglas Gillette, *King, Warrior, Magician, Lover: Rediscovering the Archetypes of the Mature Masculine* (New York: HarperCollins, 1990), 121-125.

14 David A. Rosen, *Transforming Depression: Healing the Soul Through Creativity* (New York: Penguin Group, 1993), 33-34.

15 Gregg M. Furth, *The Secret World of Drawings: Healing Through Art* (Boston, ME: Sigo Press, 1988), xiv-xix.

Chapter 2

16 C. G. Jung, *Memories, Dreams, Reflections,* ed. Aniela Jaffe, trans. Richard and Clara Winston (New York: Pantheon Books, 1963), 389.

17 Mircea Elaide, *Myth, Dreams and Mysteries,* Ed. Benjamin Nelson, trans. Philip Mairet (New York: Harper & Brothers, 1960), 156.

18 Image by Benjamin Alexander from Pixabay.

19 1909 card scanned by Holly Voley (http://home.comcast.net/~vilex/) for the public domain, and retrieved from http://www.sacred-texts.com/tarot.

20 Joseph Campbell, *Masks of God: Primitive Mythology,* vol. 1 (New York: Penguin Compass Arkana, 1991), 231.

21 Roger Canals, *A Goddess in Motion: Visual Creativity in the Cult of Maria Lionza,* ed. Jacqueline Walden, vol. 12 (New York: Berghahn, 2017), 72-75.

22 Wikipedia contributors, "María Lionza," *Wikipedia, The Free Encyclopedia,* https://en.wikipedia.org/w/index.php?title=Mar%C3%ADa_Lionza&oldid=916362848 (accessed October 4, 2019).

23 Edward F. Edinger, *The Creation of Consciousness: Jung's Myth for Modern Man* (Toronto, Canada: Inner City Books, 1984), 36-37.

24 Alice Miller, *Pictures of a Childhood: Sixty-six Watercolors and an Essay* (New York: Farrar, Straus & Giroux, 1986), 3.

25 Paul Klee, *The Diaries 1898-1918,* ed. Felix Klee (Berkely, CA: University of California Press, 1964), 249.

26 See D. W. Winnicott, *Playing and Reality* (New York: Tavistock, 1971), 12.

27 Winnicott, *Playing,* 112.

28 Daryl Sharp, *The Jung Lexicon: A Primer of Terms & Concepts* (Toronto, Canada: Inner City Books, 1991), 12.

29 Sharp, *Lexicon*, 13.

Chapter 3

30 *Merriam-Webster's Collegiate Dictionary,* 10th ed., (Springfield, MA: Merriam-Webster, Inc., 1993), s. v. "consciousness."

31 Susan Blackmore, *Consciousness: An Introduction* (New York: Oxford University Press, 2004), 25.

32 Blackmore, *Consciousness,* 14-15.

33 Antonio R. Damasio, *The Feeling of What Happens: Body and Emotion in the Making of Consciousness* (New York: Harcourt Brace, 1999), 170-171.

34 Vicki Milnark, "Mandala Therapy: Investigating Physiology, Color, and Chakras in Adults with Mood Disorders" (master's thesis, Ursuline College, 2001), 142.

35 Betty Edwards, *Drawing on the Artist Within: A Guide to Innovation, Invention, Imagination and Creativity* (New York: Simon and Schuster, 1986), 10-12.

36 Frederick Franck, *The Zen of Seeing* (New York: Alfred A. Knopf, 1973), 15.

37 Damasio, *Feeling,* 61-62.

38 Damasio, *Feeling,* 70.

39 *Merriam-Webster's Collegiate Dictionary*, 10th ed., (Springfield, MA: Merriam-Webster, Inc., 1993), s. v. "constrict."

40 *Merriam-Webster's Collegiate Dictionary*, 10th ed., (Springfield, MA: Merriam-Webster, Inc., 1993), s. v. "derelict."

41 C. G. Jung, *The Archetypes of the Collective Unconscious*, trans. R. F. C. Hull, eds., Read, Fordham and Adler, Bollinger series 20, vol. 9 (Princeton, NJ: Princeton University Press, 1969), 39.

42 Clarissa Pinkola Estés, *Women Who Run With the Wolves: Myths and Stories of the Wild Woman Archetype* (New York: Ballantine, 1992), 30-73.

43 James Hillman, *The Dream and the Underworld* (New York: Harper Perennial, 1979), 29.

44 Hillman, *Dream*, 38-41.

45 Hillman, *Dream*, 51.

46 Judith Duerk, *Circle of Stones: A Woman's Journey to Herself* (Novato, CA: New World Library), 39-40.

47 Carol Christ, *Diving Deep and Surfacing: Women Writers on a Spiritual Quest* (Boston, ME: Beacon Press, 1980) quoted in *Tsultrim* Allione, *Women of Wisdom* (Ithaca, NY: Snow Lion, 2000), 82.

Chapter 4

48 Nigel Hamilton, "The Alchemical Process of Transformation," 1985, https://www.sufismus.ch/assets/files/omega_dream/alchemy_e.pdf (accessed January 8, 2020).

49 Robert Sardello, *Love and the Soul: Creating a Future for Earth* (New York: Harper Perennial, 1996), 17-107.

50 Jean Shinoda Bolen, *Goddesses in Older Women: Archetypes in Women over Fifty* (New York: Harper Perennial, 2002), 25-34.

51 C. G. Jung, *Mysterium Coniunctionis: An Inquiry into the Separation and Synthesis of Psychic Opposites in Alchemy*, trans. R. F. C. Hull, Bollingen series 20 (Princeton, NJ: Princeton University Press, 1963), 452.

52 Alice Miller, *The Drama of the Gifted Child: The Search for the True Self*, trans. Ruth Ward (New York: Basic Books, 1981), 7.

53 C. G. Jung, *The Archetypes of the Collective Unconscious*, trans. R. F. C. Hull, eds. Read, Fordham and Adler, Bollinger series 20, vol. 9 (Princeton, NJ: Princeton University Press, 1969), 96.

54 Jung, *Archetypes*, 58-59.

55 C. G. Jung, *Psychology and Alchemy*, trans. R. F. C. Hull, Bollingen series 20, 2nd ed. (Princeton, NJ: Princeton University Press, 1953), 293.

56 M. Esther Harding, *The I and the Not-I*, 162.

57 As cited in A. Alvarez, *Night: Night Life, Night Language, Sleep and Dreams* (New York and London: W. W. Norton, 1995), 200.

58 Neil Gaiman, *Norse Mythology*, "The Treasures of the Gods" (New York: W. W. Norton & Co., 2017), 49-74.

59 Caitlin Matthews, *Sophia, Goddess of Wisdom: The Divine Feminine from the Black Goddess to the World Soul* (London: Harper Collins, 1991), 11.

60 Pat B. Allen, *Art is a Way of Knowing: A Guide to Self-knowledge and Spiritual Fulfillment Through Creativity* (Boston and London: Shambala, 1995), 165.

61 Michael C. Misja, *A Biblical Model for Hope* (Medina, OH: Eternal Press, 1995), 23.

62 See Arianna Stassinopoulos Huffington, *The Gods of Greece* (New York: Harry N. Abrams, Inc., 1983).

63 James Hillman, *Insearch: Psychology and Religion* (New York: Charles Scribner's Sons, 1967), 67.

64 Hillman, *Insearch*, 85.

Chapter 5

65 Richard Cavendish, ed., *Mythology: An Illustrated Encyclopedia* (New York: Barnes and Noble, 1993), 17-21.

66 Alain Danielou, *The Gods of India: Hindu Polytheism* (New York: Inner Traditions, 1985), 45-52.

67 Danielou, *Gods of India*, 63-69.

68 Reinhold Merkelback, "Mithraisim," Encyclopedia Britannica, Encyclopedia Britannica, Inc., December 29, 2017, https://www.britannica.com/topic/Mithraism (accessed January 9, 2020).

69 Cavendish, *Mythology*, 36.

70 John Michael Greer, *Paths of Wisdom: Principles and Practice of the Magical Cabala in the Western Tradition* (St. Paul, MN: Llewellyn, 1996), 86.

71 Robert A. Segal, *The Gnostic Jung: Selected and Introduced by Robert A. Segal* (Princeton, NJ: Princeton University Press, 1992), 207.

72 C. G. Jung, *Aion: Researches into the Phenomenology of the Self*, trans. R.F.C. Hull, 2nd ed. (Princeton, NJ: Princeton University Press, 1959), 64-65.

73 C.G. Jung, *Mysterium Coniunctionis*, 39-40.

74 Wilhelm Reich, *Character-Analysis* (New York: Farrar, Straus and Giroux, 1949), 354.

75 Reich, C*haracter*, 362.

76 Reich, C*haracter*, 311-313.

77 *Merriam-Webster's Collegiate Dictionary*, 10th ed. (Springfield, MA: Merriam-Webster, Inc., 1993), s. v. "soma."

78 Reich, C*haracter*, 358-359.

79 J. William Worden, *Grief Counseling and Grief Therapy: A Handbook for the Mental Health Practitioner*, 3rd ed. (New York: Springer, 2002), 9.

80 Worden, *Grief Counseling*, 4.

81 Worden, *Grief Counseling*, 68-69.

82 Allen, *Art is a Way*, 136.

83 Allen, *Art is a Way*, 124-125.

84 G. K. Chesterton, *The Book of Job: With an Introduction by G.K. Chesterton* (London: S. Wellwood, 1907), viii.

85 C. G. Jung, *Jung Letters*, trans. Jeffrey Hulen, ed. Gerhard Adler, vol. 2, (Princeton, NJ: Princeton University Press, 1974), 434, quoted in Edward F. Edinger, *The Creation of Consciousness: Jung's Myth for Modern Man* (Toronto, Canada: Inner City Books, 1984), 67.

86 Job 1/Hebrew-English Bible/ Mecho-Mamre, https://www.mechon-mamre.org/p/pt/pt2742.htm (accessed January 9, 2020).

87 Edinger, *Creation*, 15-17.

Chapter 6

88 Friedrich Nietzsche, *Thus Spake Zarathustra,* trans. Thomas Common (New York: Modern Library, n. d.), 23.

89 Greer, *Paths of Wisdom*, 76.

90 J. O. Urmson and Jonathan Ree, eds., *The Concise Encyclopedia of Western Philosophy* (London: Routledge, 2005), 109.

91 Viktor E. Frankl, *Man's Search for Meaning: Revised and Updated* (New York: Washington Square, 1984), 121, 131.

92 Frankl, *Search*, 141.

93 *Merriam-Webster's Collegiate Dictionary,* 10th ed. (Springfield, MA: Merriam-Webster, Inc., 1993), s. v. "courage."

94 Paul Tillich, *The Courage to Be,* 2nd ed. (New Haven, NJ: Yale University Press, 1980), 164.

95 Rollo May, *The Courage to Create* (New York: Norton, 1975), 12-14.

96 May, *Create,* 29-31.

97 Stasinopoulos Huffington, T*he Gods of Greece*, 59.

98 Jung, *Aion*, 230.

99 Jung, *Mysterium Coniunctionis,* 225.

100 Harding, *The I and the not-I*, 191.

101 Edinger, *The Creation of Consciousness*, 42.

102 Edinger, *Creation of Consciousness,* 53.

103 M. Esther Harding, *Way of All Women* (New York: Harper & Row, 1970), 203.

104 Jung, *Archetypes of the Collective Unconscious*, 235.

105 James Hillman, *A Blue Fire: Selected Writings by James Hillman*, ed. Thomas Moore (New York: Harper Perennial, 1989), 208-210.

106 Estés, *Women Who Run with the Wolves*, 28.

107 Campbell, *Primitive Mythology,* 140.

108 Danielou, *Gods of India,* 208.

109 James Frazer, *The Golden Bough: A Study of Magic and Religion* (New York: Simon and Brown, 2013), 479-501.

110 Anne Baring and Jules Cashford, *The Myth of the Goddess: Evolution of an Image* (London: Arkana, 1993), 74-75.

111 Cavendish, *Mythology,* 143.

112 Ellen Switzer and Costas, *Greek Myths: Gods, Heroes and Monsters, Their Sources, Their Stories and Their Meanings* (New York: Athenium, 1988), 36, 38.

113 Stasinopoulos Huffington, *Gods of Greece,* 97-108.

114 Harding, *Way,* 36-68.

115 Jeff A. Benner "The Ancient Hebrew Alphabet: Tav," Ancient Hebrew Research Center, https://www.ancient-hebrew.org/ancient-alphabet/tav.htm (accessed January 10, 2020).

116 Nietzsche, *Zarathustra,* 24.

117 Baring and Cashford, *Goddess,*122.

118 Nietzsche, *Zarathustra,* 24.

119 Jung, *Mysterium Coniunctionis,* 295.

120 A 1909 card scanned by Holly Voley (http://home.comcast.net/~vilex/) for the public domain, and retrieved from http://www.sacred-texts.com/tarot (see note on that page regarding source of images).

121 Wikipedia contributors, "Hexagram," *Wikipedia, The Free Encyclopedia,* https://en.wikipedia.org/w/index.php?title=Hexagram&oldid=909480673 (accessed October 1, 2019).

Chapter 7

122 Campbell, *Primitive Mythology*, 141.

123 Judith Cornell, *Mandalas: Luminous Symbols for Healing* (Wheaton, IL: Theosophical Publishing, 1994), 1.

124 Cornell, *Mandalas,* 15, 18.

125 Michael Samuels, and Mary Rockford Lane, *Creative Healing: Tapping your Hidden Creativity* (San Francisco, CA: Harper San Francisco, 1998), 49-51.

126 Samuels and Lane, *Creative Healing*, 48.

127 Don Lambert, *The Life & Art of Elizabeth "Grandma" Layton* (Waco, TX: WRS Publishing), 10-22.

128 Robert A. Segal, *The Gnostic Jung*, Gilles Quispel, "Gnosis and Psychology" (Princeton, NJ: Princeton University Press, 1992), 242.

129 Jung, *Answer to Job*, 182.

130 Wikipedia contributors, "Alfred Lawson," *Wikipedia, The Free Encyclopedia,* https://en.wikipedia.org/w/index.php?title=Alfred_Lawson&oldid=917656472 (accessed October 1, 2019).

131 Deepak Chopra, *How to Know God: The Soul's Journey into the Mystery of Mysteries* (New York: Harmony, 2000), 102.

132 Don Miguel Ruiz, *The Four Agreements Companion Book* (San Rafael, CA: Amber-Allen, 2000), 89.

133 Jung, *Psychology and Alchemy*, 301.

134 Segal, *The Gnostic Jung*, 207.

135 *Merriam-Webster's Collegiate Dictionary*, 10th ed. (Springfield, MA: Merriam-Webster, Inc., 1993), s. v. "nous."

136 Nietzsche, *Zarathustra*, 25.

137 Hillman, *A Blue Fire*, 227.

138 Harding, *The I and the Not-I*, 168.

139 Jung, *Aion*, 72-90.

140 Jung, *Aion*, 127, 134.

141 Tillich, *Be*, 105.

142 Harding, *The I and the Not-I*, 160-163.

Chapter 8

143 Kitty Belendez, "How to Grow Roses from Seed," Santa Clara Rose Society, https://scvrs.homestead.com/HybridizeKB1.html (accessed January 11, 2020).

144 Estés, *Women*, 8-9.

145 Baring and Cashford, *Goddess*, 537-564.

146 Arthur Edward Waite, *The Brotherhood of the Rosy Cross: A History of the Rosicrucians* (New York: Barnes and Noble, 1993), 88-89.

147 Demetra George, *Mysteries of the Dark Moon: The Healing Power of the Dark Goddess* (San Francisco, CA: Harper, 1992), 140-141.

148 Jung, *Mysterium Coniunctionis*, 480.

149 Rabbi Dr. Hillel ben David (Greg Killian), "The Meaning of the Number Nine (Tet)," http://betemunah.org/nine.html (accessed January 12, 2020).

150 Jung, *Mysterium Coniunctionis*, f. 221, 429, f. 222, 430.

151 Daniel C. Matt, *The Essential Kabbalah* (Edison, NJ: Castle Books, 1997), 1.

152 Matt, *Essential*, 1-2.

153 Matt, *Essential*, 66-69.

154 Segal, *The Gnostic Jung*, 181-185.

155 Jung, *Answer to Job*, 32.

156 Estés, *Women*, 9.

157 Allione, *Women of Wisdom*, 113.

158 Wikipedia contributors, "Vajrayogini," *Wikipedia, The Free Encyclopedia*, https://en.wikipedia.org/w/index.php?title=Vajrayogini&oldid=916606206 (accessed September 25, 2019).

159 Jeffrey Hopkins, *Emptiness Yoga: The Tibetan Middle Way*, ed. Joe B. Wilson (Ithaca, NY: Snow Lion, 1995), 224.

160 Sharp, *Jung Lexicon*,123

161 Sharp, *Jung Lexicon*, 97.

162 Sharp, *Jung Lexicon*, 99.

163 Edinger, *The Creation of Consciousness*, 17.

164 George, *Mysteries of the Dark Moon*, 187.

165 Bolen, *Goddesses in Older Women*, 134-141.

166 Amir Levin, M. D., and Rachel S. F. Heller, M. A., *Attached: The New Science of Adult Attachment and How it can Help you Find-and-Keep-Love* (New York: Penguin, 2010), 422-423.

167 Dee Spring, *Image and Mirage: Art Therapy with Dissociative Clients* (Springfield, IL: Charles C. Thomas, 2001), 104-109.

168 Edinger, *The Creation of Consciousness*, 9-33.

169 Jung, *Archetypes of the Collective Unconscious,* 188.

170 Jung, *Archetypes of the Collective Unconscious*, 188.

Chapter 9

171 *Merriam-Webster's Collegiate Dictionary*, 10th ed. (Springfield, MA: Merriam-Webster, Inc., 1993), s. v. "mana."

172 Owen Barfield, *Saving the Appearances: A Study in Idolatry* (New York: Harcourt, Brace and World, 1967), 111.

173 Owen Barfield, *A Barfield Reader: Selections from the Writings of Owen Barfield*, ed. G. B. Tennyson (Hanover, NH: Wesleyan University Press, 1999), xxxi-xxxii.

174 Robert A. Johnson, *Inner Work: Using Dreams and Active Imagination for Personal Growth* (New York: HarperCollins, 1989).

175 Allione, *Women of Wisdom*, 119.

176 Edith Kramer, *Art as Therapy with Children,* 2nd ed. (Chicago, IL: Magnolia Street, 1993), 10.

177 Campbell, *Primitive*, 388.

178 Campbell, *Primitive*, 328.

179 Jung, *Mysterium Coniunctionis*, 195.

180 Ruediger Dahlke, *Mandalas of the World: A Meditation and Painting Guide*, trans. Annette Englander, ed. Cornelia M. Parkinson (New York: Sterling, 1992), 46.

181 Susanne F. Fincher, *Creating Mandalas: For Insight, Healing, and Self-Expression* (Boston, MA: Shambala, 1991), 24.

182 Lauren Artress, *Walking the Sacred Path: Rediscovering the Labyrinth as a Spiritual Tool* (New York: Riverhead Books, 1995), 46-47.

183 Fincher, *Creating Mandalas,* 3.

184 Campbell, *Primitive Mythology, 240-241.*

185 Campbell, *Primitive Mythology*, 372.

BIOGRAPHY

Vicki Lynn Milnark, born in Cleveland, Ohio, is third generation Finnish, Irish and Italian. Raised on a farm, she rode horseback and attended art club in high school. She wrote in a journal since her teenage years. She also was a reporter for a weekly newspaper while in college and later began writing poetry. Because of Carl Jung's literature, Milnark recorded dreams for over thirty years. She also painted or drew dreams and created numerous visual journals.

As a nuclear medicine technologist for twenty-five years, she supported her children. A voice in a dream told her to paint which led to vocation as an art therapist. She therefore completed a master's degree in art therapy at Ursuline College in 2001, launching into a second career at midlife. Her thesis, *Mandala therapy: Investigating physiology, color, and chakras in adults with mood disorders*, (2001) won the Thesis Design Award. Milnark obtained her counseling license in 2005.

She has eighteen years' experience as a counselor and art therapist in a variety of settings with children and adults. Those include a renal care facility, elementary schools, a senior center, individual art therapy for adolescents, and medical art therapy. Further, she became employed by a hospice facility as a bereavement coordinator and started an art therapy program with the terminally ill. At the IOP, she assisted in the development of the Dialectical Behavior Therapy (DBT) program and later created an Acceptance and Commitment Therapy (ACT) program using art therapy over an eleven-year period. She was in private practice for five years.

Akin to professional life, Milnark won first prize for drawing and an honorable mention for painting at Lakeland

Community College. She volunteered for Seasons of Life Hospice and sat as bylaws chair for the Buckeye Art Therapy Association. She is a member of the American Art Therapy Association, the Buckeye Art Therapy Association, Jung Cleveland and a book discussion group of Jungian authors. Newly retired, Milnark attends figure drawing classes and continues to write, and to record and sometimes, draw dreams. She lives with her partner in Parma, Ohio.

www.ingramcontent.com/pod-product-compliance
Lightning Source LLC
LaVergne TN
LVHW090939080826
845145LV00003B/818